Men-at-Arms • 19

The Iron Brigade

John Selby • Illustrated by Michael Roffe
Series editor Martin Windrow

First published in Great Britain in 1971 by Osprey Publishing,
Midland House, West Way, Botley, Oxford OX2 0PH, UK
44-02 23rd St, Suite 219, Long Island City, NY 11101, USA
Email: info@ospreypublishing.com

© 1971 Osprey Publishing Ltd.

All rights reserved. Apart from any fair dealing for the purpose of private study, research, criticism or review, as permitted under the Copyright, Designs and Patents Act, 1988, no part of this publication may be reproduced, stored in a retrieval system, or transmitted in any form or by any means, electronic, electrical, chemical, mechanical, optical, photocopying, recording or otherwise, without the prior written permission of the copyright owner. Enquiries should be addressed to the Publishers.

Transferred to digital print on demand 2010

First published 1971
3rd impression 2004

Printed and bound by Cadmus Communications, USA

A CIP catalog record for this book is available from the British Library

ISBN: 978 0 85045 054 5

Index by Peter Rea

Acknowledgements
The author is indebted to *The Iron Brigade* by Alan T. Nolan (New York, 1961) for details of the exploits of the Brigade, and wishes also to thank Mr Nolan for help with the pictures.

FOR A CATALOG OF ALL BOOKS PUBLISHED BY
OSPREY MILITARY AND AVIATION PLEASE CONTACT:

Osprey Direct, c/o Random House Distribution Center,
400 Hahn Road, Westminster, MD 21157
Email: uscustomerservice@ospreypublishing.com

Osprey Direct, The Book Service Ltd, Distribution Centre,
Colchester Road, Frating Green, Colchester, Essex, CO7 7DW
Email: customerservice@ospreypublishing.com

www.ospreypublishing.com

The Iron Brigade

Bull Run

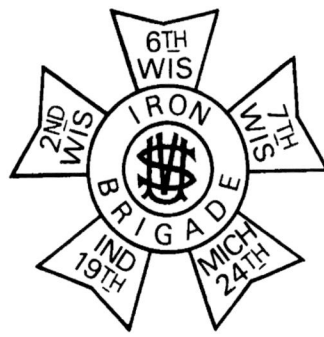

Although Wisconsin's quota included only one infantry regiment, the response to the Governor's call to arms was so enthusiastic that additional regiments, including the Second Wisconsin Volunteers, were formed; and on 16 May 1861, little more than a month after the first mortar shell which signalled the start of the war burst over Fort Sumter, the Regiment's ten companies assembled at Madison and were mustered into the United States' service for three years.

The people of the North clamoured for a quick march on the Southern capital to end the war. 'On to Richmond!' was their cry; and this popular pressure persuaded General McDowell to launch a drive south prematurely.

The best route to Richmond from Washington was along the railroad through Manassas Junction, for with good supporting roads it assured an overland approach that avoided many of the natural barriers found on the shorter route by Fredericksburg, where the Occoquan and Aquia creeks and the Rappahannock River had to be crossed.

Realizing the strategic importance of Manassas, the Confederate commander, General Beauregard, drew up and partially entrenched his forces along Bull Run which ran like a ditch of a fortress across his front.

On 25 June 1861 the Second Wisconsin joined General Irvin McDowell at Washington, and on 16 July he led his army straight down the Centreville-Warrenton turnpike towards General Beauregard's defence line. The advance was ponderous throughout. The regiments left Washington brilliantly uniformed, some like the Second Wisconsin in Volunteer grey, some in Federal blue, some in gaudy Zouave dress copying the French; and their silk banners flung to the breeze were unsoiled and untorn. But the men were still mostly civilians in uniform, who like the Second Wisconsin had been under arms for only two months. Unused to marching, by the time they reached Centreville they were hot, weary, bedraggled and footsore,

General Irvin McDowell, Commander of the Federal forces at First Bull Run

Federal forces in camp outside Washington at the beginning of the war

and dropped down as soon as they halted. Another cause of delay was the throng of visitors from Washington, official and unofficial, who came in carriages to see the fun, and cluttered up roads which should have been reserved for troop movements.

After the Federal vanguard had been repulsed at Blackburn's Ford, General McDowell stopped to consolidate and plan a turning movement round Beauregard's position in the north. By the morning of 21 July the Federals were on the move again, and McDowell stood at the point on the turnpike where his flanking columns turned to the right, and watched his men pass. He gazed silently and with evident pride upon the regiments as they filed by, lively again in the freshness of the morning. Later he conducted with some success the northern battle in which his forces drove the Confederates on Matthews Hill back over Young's Branch to Henry House Hill. Here, however, the Confederates rallied, and were reinforced with troops from the Shenandoah Valley brought by rail to Manassas Junction – troops which included the formidable First Virginian Brigade under General Jackson.

Meanwhile, a frontal attack by General Tyler's First Division down the turnpike on Stone Ridge was developing. This secondary assault fared better than had been anticipated, for General Sherman's brigade in which the Second Wisconsin served found a ford to the north of Stone Bridge, and after crossing were able to move up the track from Stone House and join in the attack on Henry House Hill alongside their fellows who had gone round the Confederate's north flank – see map 1.

Sherman ordered his men to attack the now formidable Confederate defence line stretching across Henry House Hill. Fighting his brigade by regiments, he sent forward first the Second Wisconsin and then the Thirteenth, Seventy-ninth and Sixty-ninth New York regiments of his brigade. Of the Wisconsins he wrote:

'The roadway up Henry House Hill was worn deep enough to afford shelter, and I kept the several regiments on it as long as possible, but when the Wisconsin 2nd was abreast of the enemy, by order of Major Wadsworth of General McDowell's staff I ordered it to leave the roadway by the left flank to attack the enemy. This regiment ascended to the brow of the hill steadily, received the severe fire of the enemy, returned it with spirit and advanced delivering its fire. This regiment was uniformed in grey cloth almost identical with that of the great bulk of the secession army, and when the regiment fell into confusion and retreated towards the road, there was a universal cry that they were being fired on by their own men. The regiment rallied again, passed the brow of the hill a second time, but was again repulsed.'

Finally, along with the rest of McDowell's troops attacking Henry House Hill they were swept off by a Confederate counter-attack. A brief rally north of Young's Branch was broken up by Confederate artillery, after which there was

This is what the Second Wisconsin Volunteers looked like on mustering. 'A few wore broadcloth and silk hats, more the red shirts of raftsmen, several were in country homespun, and one had a calico coat'

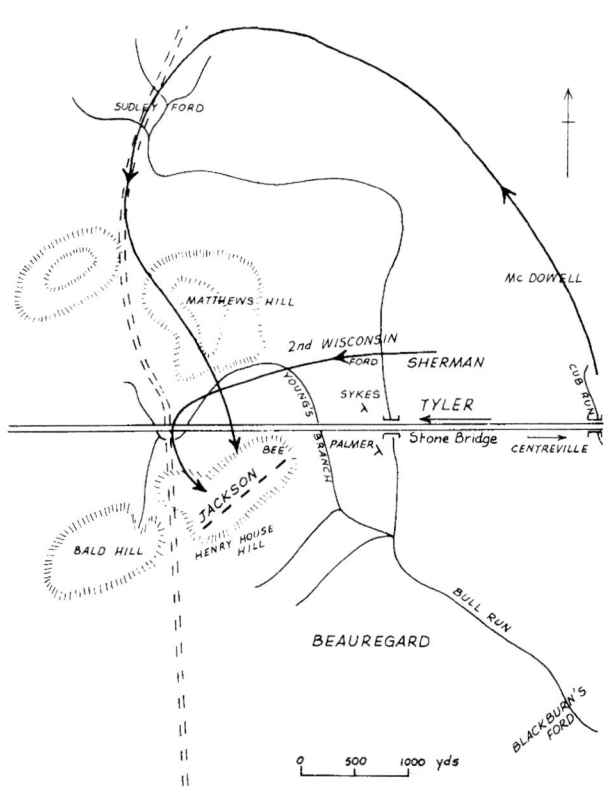

1 **Battle of First Bull Run**

Frederick's Hall Raid

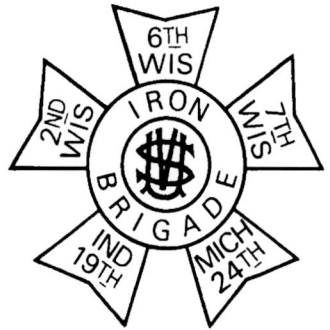

In July 1861 after the battle at Bull Run the Second Wisconsin were transferred to the brigade of Rufus King, joining the Sixth Wisconsin and Nineteenth Indiana at Washington. During their time in the capital the Second Wisconsin were employed across the Chain Bridge in Virginia constructing earthworks to cover its approaches. The Sixth Wisconsin were first issued with an all-grey short-jacketed uniform similar to that worn by the Second at Bull Run. When the Sixth paraded to receive it they looked a rather odd lot: 'A few wore broadcloth and silk hats, more the red shirts of raftsmen, several were in country homespun, one had a calico coat, and another was looking through the hole in the drooping brim of a straw hat.' On 23 August 1861 they were reviewed by General Rufus King, but were disappointed in their performance, for their band played so slowly that they 'had to hold one leg in the air and balance on the other while they waited for the music'. Early in August 1861 the Nineteenth Indiana arrived in Washington clad in 'gray doeskin cassimere and carrying Enfield or Minié rifles'. The Seventh Wisconsin arrived on 1 October 1861. Governor Randall of Wisconsin had planned to form an all-Wisconsin brigade to send east, but the Nineteenth Indiana remained with the three Wisconsin regiments and were later joined by the Twenty-fourth Michigan. These regiments of what came to be called the Iron Brigade were largely country boys from farms and small towns. A small majority were native-born Americans;

a general retreat over Stone Bridge towards home, covered by Sykes's regulars of the Second Division and Palmer's cavalry. A shot from a Confederate battery hit the bridge over Cub Run, upsetting a wagon which had just driven upon it. This blocked the bridge and caused panic and confusion which was increased by the throngs of sightseers also making their way back to Washington along the crowded narrow roads. All through the night and rain of the next day the soldiers and civilians stormed into Washington. Attempts by General McDowell to rally his soldiers were in vain. But the exhausted battle-weary Confederates made no effective pursuit. The Confederate cavalry did succeed in capturing a number of prisoners, but the main Union forces escaped. By 22 July both armies were back in the position they had occupied prior to the battle.

Rufus King, the first Commander of the Iron Brigade, and Divisional Commander at the Battle of Brawner Farm (State Historical Society of Wisconsin)

Irishmen and Scandinavians accounted for some 40 per cent; and the remainder were Germans with a few Englishmen and Canadians. In October a regular artillery battery was attached. This was Battery B commanded by Major John Gibbon. As it was short of almost half its complement of 152, General McClellan authorized Major Gibbon to visit the other regiments of McDowell's Division to pick more artillerymen; and he chose them mainly either from the New York regiments or from King's regiments. Later more of King's men went into Battery B, and such transfers from the personnel of the Brigade were to continue throughout the long and happy association. Battery B had been formed in 1821 and had fought with distinction in the Florida War of 1837 and the Mexican War of 1845. It was a model for the Brigade to try to emulate.

From Washington the Brigade was moved to Falmouth on the north side of the Rappahannock from Fredericksburg, where it was in the front line between the two warring armies; but, nevertheless, it did not participate in General McClellan's Peninsular Campaign, or in any of the fierce Seven Days' Battles near Richmond of June and July 1862. At Falmouth General Rufus King, on promotion to divisional commander, handed over command to John Gibbon of Battery B. The new leader immediately set about introducing the strict discipline of this famous battery, and he must get much of the credit for the high degree of military efficiency which the Brigade achieved. He also obtained the new and distinctive uniform for which they are renowned. In September 1861 all the regiments had drawn ordinary Federal dark blue uniforms to replace their grey ones. Now, in May 1862, they were equipped in dark blue single-breasted frock-coats, with light blue collar trim, reaching almost to the knees, and light blue trousers; also white leggings; and in place of the *képi*, the black felt Hardee hat of the regulars. This hat, often punched up high, gave them their popular name of 'the Black Hats'. It was a most suitable garb for a brigade which, though composed of volunteers, was to become the First Brigade of the First Division of the First Corps, and to prove great fighters.

On 26 June 1862 President Lincoln consolidated the armies scattered around Washington into the Army of Virginia, and placed them under the command of General John Pope who had led successful operations in the West. Lincoln next planned another direct assault on Richmond but, before it began, a series of intelligence and probing missions were carried out. General King's division of McDowell's Corps, in which the Brigade served, was anxious about a reported Confederate concentration in the Gordonsville area, and he ordered Gibbon to take a mixed column of cavalry, infantry and artillery to investigate. They moved out from Falmouth, crossed the river to Fredericksburg and then took the Plank Road through Chancellorsville, going nearly to Orange Court House. Here they learnt from the inhabitants that a large force under General Stonewall Jackson had arrived in the vicinity. After skirmishing with some Confederate cavalry, they withdrew to present this valuable piece of information to General King.

On 3 August 1862 McClellan was directed to evacuate the peninsula east of Richmond and

John Gibbon, the second Commander of the Iron Brigade, who can be considered its creator as a distinctive unit. He fostered its special fighting qualities and gave the Brigade its well-known dress. He led the Brigade through its spectacular engagements in the summer and autumn of 1862 after being promoted from the command of Battery B (National Archives)

unite his Army of the Potomac with Pope's Army of Virginia. In the meantime, Pope was ordered to strike at the Confederate lines of communication between Richmond and Gordonsville, and hamper the Confederate build-up in the Gordonsville area. With this in view, on 5 August 1862, a large-scale raid, in which the Brigade participated, was mounted on Frederick's Hall Station midway between Richmond and Gordonsville – see map 2.

Gibbon's Brigade led the way, and was followed by Hatch's Brigade. Gibbon divided his force. Colonel Cutler and the Sixth Wisconsin with a squadron of cavalry and two guns moved west through Chancellorsville by the Plank Road and then turned south towards Spottsylvania and Frederick's Hall Station. Gibbon and the other three regiments with the Third Indiana Cavalry and a battery took the Telegraph Road south direct for Frederick's Hall. Fifteen miles south of Fredericksburg at Thornburg, Gibbon brushed with Confederate cavalry, and thereupon sent off a dispatch to Cutler to warn him of their presence. Meanwhile Gibbon's men opened fire and drove the cavalry off; but most of the contingent was by this time so prostrated by the heat that Gibbon thought it advisable to delay the advance until the next day. Even so, he had to leave behind 70 men with Hatch's Brigade which had by this time reached Thornburg and encamped there.

They had not gone far on the road to Frederick's Hall Station next day before a cavalry scout returned with a dispatch reporting that General Jeb Stuart with a large enemy force was now in their rear. Fearing being cut off from his base, Gibbon decided to retreat, and when he reached Hatch's camp found his fellow brigadier was already engaging some of Stuart's horsemen.

On the following morning, still skirmishing with Stuart, Gibbon moved his force to the Plank Road to protect Cutler's retreat. He need not have done this. Cutler, bolder than his brigade commander, despite the warning message, was already on his way to carry out the mission.

Reaching the North Anna, Cutler left a detachment under Captain Plummer to guard the wooden bridge which so easily might be burnt and stop them returning over the unfordable stream. Then, having filled their canteens and left their excess equipment in Plummer's camp, the remainder crossed the 150-foot bridge span 40 feet above the water-level. Two miles from Frederick's Hall Station Cutler sent forward the cavalry who

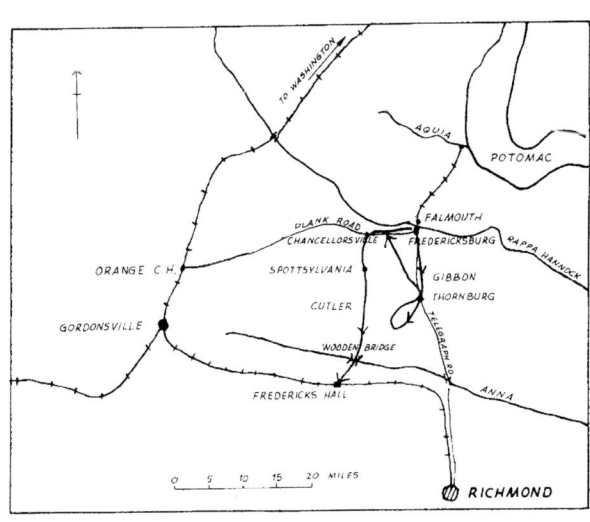

2 The raid on Frederick's Hall Station

7

The black felt Hardee hat. When worn by the regulars the brim was turned up on the left side and fastened with a brass eagle pin. The Iron Brigade gave it a few special characteristics by turning the brim either up or down, on either side, according to the wearer's fancy. When the crown lost its shape they tended to punch it up instead of allowing it to slouch. The plume was worn on either side, and not always replaced when lost or worn out. However the light blue hat cord and the brass horn were almost always retained; and in addition the brass company letter was worn – see colour plates

swooped into the village, cut the telegraph wires, picketed the roads and began the destruction of the railroad. Next, the infantry and artillery moved in, and after posting the guns to cover the approaches and part of the infantry to protect the village from attack, the rest joined the cavalry in the task of destruction. By six in the evening all the whisky and corn in the village belonging to the Confederate Army had been destroyed, and two miles of railroad track ripped up. With their

Stragglers at the rear of the column. Fifty-nine men were captured by straggling after the raid on Frederick's Hall, but after this the Brigade became famous for not straggling

mission completed the column returned, crossed the river by the bridge and rejoined Plummer's men in camp. Here Cutler received a second dispatch from Gibbon reporting Stuart's presence. Weary though they still were, therefore, early next morning Colonel Cutler had his force on the road again. They came up with Gibbon's men near Spottsylvania, and there the united column camped for the night before returning to Fredericksburg and Falmouth next day.

So ended the first engagement of the Brigade. Colonel Cutler's contingent had done splendidly. But all the results were not so satisfactory. Gibbon had to report the loss of 59 men from his brigade, exhausted men who had straggled and been captured by Confederate cavalry. But the others learned the lesson that to straggle was to be lost, and the Brigade later became renowned for not straggling.

Groveton

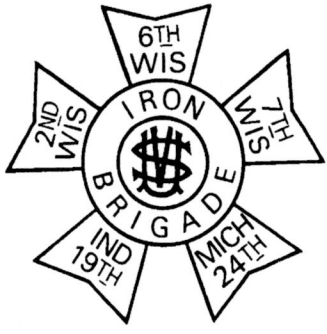

General Pope's advance south was soon brought to a halt. The Federals were moving by Army Corps and were well separated. They planned to concentrate about Culpeper Court House between the Rappahannock and Rapidan, but advanced elements of General Banks's II Army Corps were already beyond the court house, and this gave the Confederates their opportunity. A force under General Jackson moved quickly northwards and struck at and defeated Banks's advanced troops at Cedar Run before they could be reinforced; after which Jackson fell back again to the area of Clark's Mountain south of the Rapidan.

While this was happening, Gibbon's Brigade

was still at Falmouth; but they afterwards moved west to bury the dead of Cedar Run, and when Pope moved all his army back to the north of the Rappahannock, the Brigade went to Rappahannock Station where the railway crosses the river. For a time the front line between the armies was the Rappahannock, and small raids were carried out by both sides over it; but there soon followed some of the most spectacular Confederate manœuvres of the whole war. Jeb Stuart took his horsemen along the west bank of the Rappahannock, crossed near Waterloo, and moved behind the rear of Pope's armies manning the Rappahannock. His objective was Catlett's Station on the main railroad to Washington. There he attempted, and failed, to destroy the railroad bridge, but managed to cut the telegraph wires and set the camp ablaze. He returned with 300 prisoners and several valuable mounts. This, however, was only the beginning. On the next raid Jackson took his whole corps up the same route as Stuart, but went as far north as Salem before turning east down the railroad through Thoroughfare Gap. Proceeding as far as Manassas Junction, he laid waste the main Federal base store there. After which he fell back to a strong defence position on Stony Bridge north of Groveton, near the field of battle of First Bull Run.

Pope was now thoroughly apprehensive about what was happening in his rear and started moving back his army corps from the Rappahannock to deal with the raiders. During this reorganization Gibbon's Brigade was ordered to leave Rappahannock Station and march north down the Warrenton Turnpike past Stone Bridge to Centreville; and short of the bridge at Brawner Farm near Groveton they were to fight a spirited action.

As Gibbon's soldiers proceeded on their way through the peaceful countryside Jackson, having placed his men in strong defensive positions on Stony Ridge, rode forward with some of his officers to reconnoitre. Leaving his officers in the wood, he went on alone to its forward edge behind Brawner Farm, and from his vantage-point, was amazed to see Federal forces marching obliviously along the turnpike a few hundred yards in front of him. This was too great an opportunity to miss. Wheeling his horse, he returned to the group of officers. Touching his hat in military salute, he said in as soft a voice as if he had been talking to a friend in ordinary conversation, 'Bring out your men, Gentlemen!' Every officer wheeled and scurried back through the woods at full gallop, and the battle at Brawner Farm began.

Up to this time General Gibbon had been unaware of the danger facing his brigade, for although the Confederates had now left their wooded hiding-place, they were hidden in a dip between the wood and the ridge on which Brawner Farm stood. However, when Gibbon and the head of his brigade on the road reached the eastern edge of the rectangular wood just beyond the entrance to Brawner Farm, they saw what appeared to be the horses of a gun team coming into action at the top of an open field. Friend or foe? Leaving the road Gibbon went forward along the edge of the wood to a knoll to investigate, and soon realized that a Confederate battery was coming into action, and was about to shell his column. Gibbon reacted quickly. He ordered Battery B to be brought up from the rear of the column to silence the Confederate battery; and when they arrived, eager hands tore down the turnpike fence and the guns passed into the field and came into action by the knoll from which Gibbon had watched the enemy. By this time Confederate shells were screaming overhead and bursting all about, so Gibbon decided to attack the enemy on Brawner Farm ridge without further delay. On his orders, the Sixth Wisconsin wheeled round the eastern edge of the wood, the Second and Seventh passed back through its south-west corner to attack Brawner Farm's buildings directly, and the Nineteenth Indiana left the road and moved against the western edge of Brawner ridge. Meanwhile, realizing the great strength of the Confederate force opposing him, Gibbon dispatched requests for assistance to his divisional commander Rufus King; but no help came except that, as a result of a direct appeal, General Doubleday sent two regiments.

The battle was now joined, and from first to last continued unabated for more than two hours. It was a stand-up fight at a maximum range of seventy-five yards, with no respite and neither side entrenched or under cover. The Confederates for a time advanced a few yards, reached the zigzag fence along the north side of the wood and forced

Colonel O'Connor (right) at a meal in the headquarters mess of the Second Wisconsin Volunteers. He was mortally wounded at the Battle of Groveton

Doubleday's regiments back. Meanwhile, an advance by the Nineteenth Indiana on the west end of the ridge was held by the Confederates. But except for these movements neither side advanced or retreated, and the Confederates held fast to the farmhouse and the northern edge of the orchard about it, and Gibbon's men the farmyard, the southern edge of the orchard and their line along the zigzag fence on the northern face of the wood. The fiercest actions took place around the farm buildings. Gibbon never left this part of the line, 'and there the feverish and bloody action reached its climax amidst the roar of musketry fire and the shouts and cheers of the soldiers'. Gibbon later said it was the fiercest musketry fire that he had ever listened to, and a Confederate considered it 'one of the most terrific conflicts' and that the 'black-hatted' fellows had taken a terrible toll of them. The fight continued until dark when it was left as a drawn battle and both sides withdrew; Gibbon to report to Rufus King, who immediately ordered all his forces in the area to fall back to Manassas and leave the conduct of the coming assault on Jackson's main position on Stony Ridge to their army commander General Pope. An English commentator confirmed that the battle ended as a draw, but added that 'the men who faced each other that August evening fought with a gallantry that has seldom been surpassed'. Gibbon was justly proud of his volunteer brigade. As of ten days previously he had referred to them as 'green', now he kept exclaiming how proud he was to be commanding them. It certainly was a bloody affair. Many distinguished Confederates fell including General Ewell, who later lost a leg from his wound, and General Taliaferro who was forced to relinquish command of the Jackson Division. On the Federal side, Colonel O'Connor of the Second Wisconsin fell mortally wounded, Colonel Cutler of the Sixth was wounded in the leg and carried from the field by his horse, and Colonel Robinson of the Seventh

Wisconsin and the Colonel of the Fifty-sixth Pennsylvania were wounded. In all, the losses of the six Federal regiments engaged amounted to 912, and of the Confederates some 2,000.

From the Battle of Groveton Pope had discovered the position of the Confederates. He had already sent Ricketts's Division to watch Thoroughfare Gap and stop reinforcements reaching Jackson on Stony Ridge, now he planned to concentrate on either side of Jackson and crush him before 'by any possibility reinforcements could reach the scene of action'. Pope's plan was sound enough, but its execution went sadly awry. McDowell's Corps was too strung out to be concentrated readily, and the other commanders, particularly General Porter, were hard to persuade to take their corps into the fight where they were required. The result was that the Federal frontal attacks on Stony Ridge were first delayed and then went in piecemeal, and General Longstreet's Corps coming through Thoroughfare Gap, having brushed aside Rickett's men, was able to form up well forward on Jackson's western flank. This folding round the Federals by Longstreet's men proved to be the battle-winning factor. First his guns and then his infantrymen struck at the flanks of the Federal troops attacking Jackson on Stony Ridge, and eventually swept them from the field of battle.

Gibbon's men did not enter the fray until the second day. They moved into battle through a wood behind two other brigades of their division, the Nineteenth Indiana in the centre, the consolidated Second and Seventh Wisconsin on the left and the Sixth Wisconsin on the right. The wood was so overgrown that the officers had to dismount, and as they picked their way through the trees furious enfilade fire from Longstreet's guns struck them. Ahead, the leading brigades reached the far edge of the wood, and through the smoke and fire could be seen their objective. Directly in front was a rail fence, beyond the fence an open field, and beyond that the unfinished railroad embankment – a wall of earth 15 feet high. Crowning the embankment were the musket barrels and slouch hats of Ewell's Division, Gibbon's adversaries of two days before at Brawner Farm. The leaders climbed the rail fence, and with a shout rushed forward. They were met with a withering fire which included shot and shell from Longstreet's guns on the left. The odds were too great. A few valiant spirits reached the embankment only to be battered with stones thrown by the Confederates and fired into by their Federal comrades from behind; the rest were driven back. As they retreated in confusion on to those behind, this second brigade began to disintegrate and join them in flight. In their retrograde movement the two disordered brigades ran into Gibbon's line, and the Wisconsin and Indiana soldiers received a strange new command from their general, revolver in hand. 'Stop these stragglers,' he cried. 'Shoot them if they won't stop!' In response to the bayonets of Gibbon's Brigade and the feverish activities of their own

Stone Bridge after the Battle of Second Bull Run. 'The road was almost blocked by a slowly moving mass of stragglers, wagons, artillery, ambulances and wounded, some of whom were being borne in hand litters'

officers, the broken brigades rallied; but the Federal attack was beaten, and a general withdrawal was ordered to the higher ground in the rear.

Now it was the Confederates' turn. Before the Federals could recover from their bloody repulse, Jackson's line moved forward and Longstreet's divisions swept in from the flank. Gibbon's soldiers hugged the ground, harassed by a galling artillery fire and watched Battery B respond on their behalf. But this passive role ended as Jackson's men at last emerged from the wood to Gibbon's front and came into range. At the first appearance of Stonewall's men, Gibbon mistook them for Federals retreating from the wood where

Company I of the Seventh Wisconsin, photographed at Upton's Hill, September 1862

they had been so recently engaged, and told his people to hold their fire. But a German captain of artillery soon put him wise, and then the Federal artillery and infantry opened up, tearing great gaps in the Confederate line. They could not hold them back for long, however, for on the left Longstreet's Corps overran Bald Hill, and a grey tide swept round the base of Henry House Hill threatening the rear of the blue line along the turnpike, so Pope ordered a general retreat.

Gibbon's Brigade was assigned to cover this movement, and the Western men established their line beside the Warrenton Turnpike on the north face of Henry House Hill with Battery B unlimbered in action in support. In the deepening darkness the battle died away, but officers' commands could still be heard, and cannon fire in the distance. Finally, the Brigade and Battery B fell in on the turnpike for the march to the rear. Here it was First Bull Run all over again. At Stone Bridge overturned wagons gave the Wisconsin and Indiana soldiers a welcome supply of bread, but on crossing the bridge Gibbon found the road almost blocked by a slowly moving mass of stragglers, wagons, artillery, ambulances and wounded, some of whom were being borne by their comrades in hand litters. The Brigade followed the turnpike to Cub Run, two miles beyond Stone Bridge, and there Gibbon directed his staff to put them into camp.

Although the Westerners had been on the fringe of the battle of the last two days, 15 more men were dead, 87 wounded and 47 missing, most of them in the wood. Including the losses of Brawner Farm, 900 of Gibbon's men were casualties.

The Maryland Campaign

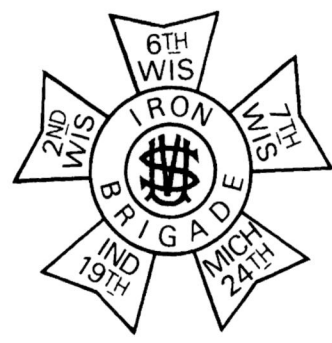

After Second Bull Run Pope's armies withdrew into the defence system of Washington, and McClellan was assigned by President Lincoln to the command. There was little call for reliance on McClellan after his failure in the Peninsular Campaign, but the public still believed in him – and the army, for on hearing the good news Gibbon's Brigade threw their black hats in the air.

Meanwhile Lee decided with the approval of President Jefferson Davis to cross the Potomac and enter Maryland. Parts of Maryland were sympathetic, and it was thought that the presence of the Southern Army might induce Maryland to ally herself with the South. Lee also hoped to recruit men for his armies, and obtain supplies of food and clothing. By moving north Lee thought that he could draw the Federals away from Richmond, and keep their armies on their own side of the Potomac.

After crossing the Potomac Lee established his headquarters at Frederick, but the reception his army received in Maryland was by no means enthusiastic so he withdrew westwards to Sharpsburg followed closely, but not very rapidly, by McClellan. Two lines of hills lay athwart Lee's march westwards, and in the gaps of the second range sharp rearguard actions were fought. At Turner's Gap by South Mountain Gibbon's Brigade was engaged.

Three roads ran through separate defiles in Turner's Gap: the Old Hagerstown Road, the National Road and the Sharpsburg Road. Two corps under Hooker and Reno with Burnside in overall control were assigned to move up these roads, and Gibbon's Brigade, as part of Hooker's force, had the task of clearing the National Road in the centre, well in view of their comrades to right and left. Meanwhile, a mixed force under General Longstreet awaited them in the gorge.

When Gibbon's Brigade were halted in a field off the road, waiting the order to advance, they could see two miles to their right their comrades on the Old Hagerstown Road, 'long lines and heavy columns of dark blue infantry pressing up the green slopes of the mountain, their bayonets flashing like silver in the rays of the sun'. About the same distance to their left on the Sharpsburg Road Reno's men were moving forward. The flank assaults had begun.

The opposing Confederates, taking advantage of natural cover, fought with great determination; but the Federals ground slowly ahead up the rugged mountainside, impeded but never checked by the plunging fire of their adversaries. At last, after an hour's wait, and just as the sun began to sink behind the mountain summit, a dispatch rider reached Gibbon with the order to attack.

Gibbon first deployed his skirmishers and then sent out behind them the Indiana to the left and the Seventh Wisconsin to the right. Following the leading regiments at 200 yards distance came the Second Wisconsin behind the Indiana, and the Sixth Wisconsin behind the Seventh, while two of Battery B's guns came into action on the road. With a cheer they were off, and passed quickly through a slight dip before starting the ascent into the mountain gorge. Mounted on his horse, Gibbon rode with the front line, exhorting the Westerners with the repeated command of 'Forward!'

As the men began their climb, they were at once fired at by the enemy from behind logs and bushes, from farm buildings and finally from behind a stone fence on the left of the road; but they pressed on regardless. When a wood on the right exploded with a deadly fire, there was grim execution among the Seventh, its color disappearing and reappearing as one color-bearer after another was shot down. When the sadly depleted ranks reached the defenders' main line

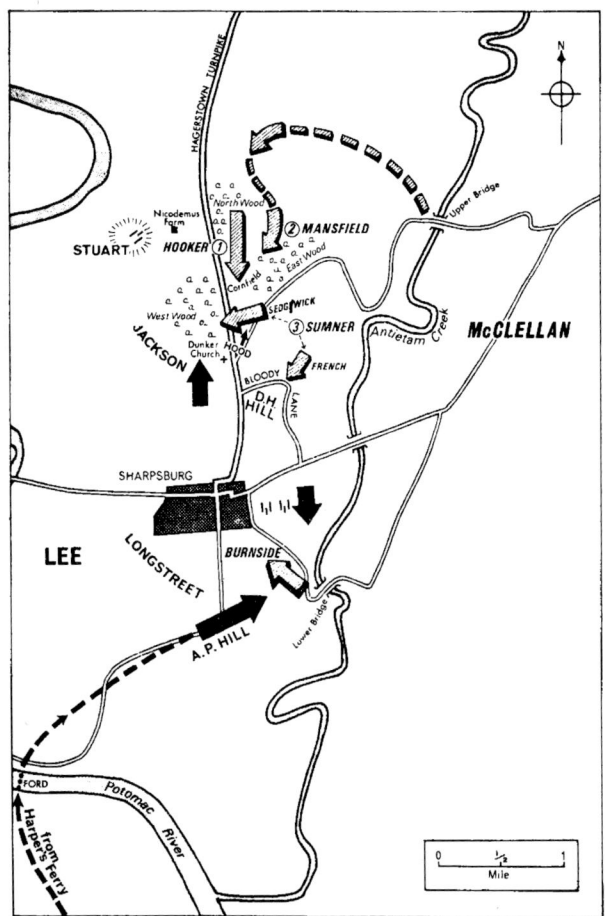

3 The Battle of Antietam or Sharpsburg, 17 September 1862

at the apex of the pass 1,000 rifles poured down from a stone wall, lighting up the gathering darkness. This halted the Federal advance, and a deadly pitched battle for the wall ensued in which all Battery B's guns joined. An attempt at outflanking the wall was only partially successful owing to a temporary shortage of ammunition so Gibbon ordered the ground won to be held with the bayonet. There followed a Confederate bayonet charge met by an advance, with bayonets fixed, by the Brigade, which drove the enemy behind their stone barricade again. Soon the defenders of the wall were also suffering from want of ammunition. Their firing gradually died down, then ceased. As darkness fell they slipped away, and the battle was won.

During the night Gibbon counted his losses, and found he had suffered 318 casualties with 37 dead, the Seventh Wisconin, who had fronted the deadly stone wall, suffering most. But the gallant manner in which the Brigade fought had not passed unnoticed. General McClellan officially reported that 'their bravery could not have been excelled', and General Hooker spoke of them as his 'iron brigade'. This was received by the Westerners with great satisfaction, and from then on they became 'The Iron Brigade'.

After the battle at Turner's Gap John Gibbon led the Iron Brigade through the II Corps troops still lying near the gorge and rejoined his own I Corps. Meanwhile, Lee had established himself in a formidable defensive position behind Antietam Creek on either side of the town of Sharpsburg with his right flank protected by the Potomac. Antietam Creek, although shallow, formed an obstacle to McClellan's advance, and largely confined him to the bridges for his crossings. McClellan's plan was a double envelopment with General Burnside's Corps attacking over Lower Bridge in the south, and Hooker's, Mansfield's and Sumner's Corps crossing in succession at Upper Bridge, and coming down from the north – see map 3. The most powerful thrust was therefore in the north, where Hooker's Corps, who were leading, with the Iron Brigade in front, drove down the Hagerstown Turnpike, past Miller Farm, through West Woods and the Cornfield to meet the full force of the Confederates east of Dunker Church.

To drive the enemy from West Woods, Gibbon ordered the Seventh Wisconsin and Nineteenth Indiana to leave the turnpike and deploy by the barns of Miller Farm which were on the west of the road. Here they were joined by two guns of Battery B. Meanwhile the Sixth – less some companies with the Seventh – and the Second Wisconsin took the east side of the road. As the right wing scrambled over the zigzag fence into West Woods, the left wing entered the Cornfield and were lost to view.

At once, the Confederate lines of infantry and artillery exploded, and a terrible carnage followed. To the west of the turnpike the Nineteenth and Seventh supported by the guns of Battery B ground slowly forward through West Woods, the men of Jackson's Division falling back, or retreating across the turnpike to the cover of the Cornfield. On the Cornfield side it was more difficult. It was but 1,000 yards from the front edge of the

14

field to Dunker Church, its white walls backed by the green of West Woods behind. Driving out from the trees came the Nineteenth Indiana and Seventh Wisconsin, and over the far Cornfield fence went the Sixth and Second racing for the church. But the Confederates rallied and drove the Federals back into the woods and over the Cornfield fence. Back and forth the tide of battle went until at one stage the church was only 200 yards away from the Iron Brigade closing in on both sides of the turnpike. The Confederates started to trickle away, their ammunition exhausted. For the Federals the day was almost won. But it was not won. Suddenly appeared a long steady line of grey sweeping from the woods behind the church. It was Hood's Brigade, and other fresh Confederate troops. Before this new assault the Federal line faltered, and then drew back through the Cornfield. At the northern edge every color-bearer and member of the color-guard of the Sixth was killed, and Major Rufus Dawes seized the colors himself and rallied his men. To

The attack at Dunker Church; and a photograph taken afterwards. Of the 800 infantrymen who entered this battle, 342 were casualties. (Library of Congress)

his right John Gibbon, dismounted and grimed in black with powder and smoke, laboured with Battery B, aiming one gun himself with the cry, 'Give 'em hell, boys!' In the wild tumult before the Confederates closed, Gibbon, aware that his men were almost out of ammunition, extricated them skilfully. Although some guns had but two horses, not a gun or wagon was left behind. His infantry did not, however, fare as well. Of the 800 who entered the battle 342 were casualties.

The Brigade was again highly complimented for its part in the battle by the Commander-in-Chief who is recorded as saying that they reflected the greatest credit on themselves and 'were equal to the best troops in any army in the world'.

Hooker's attack having failed, the other corps following him over Upper Bridge were also held by the Confederates with great slaughter on both sides. Finally, Burnside, belatedly crossing Lower Bridge, was struck in the flank by A. P. Hill's force returning from capturing Harper's Ferry, and the whole Federal Army pulled back and allowed Lee to take his army to Virginia at his leisure.

Fredericksburg

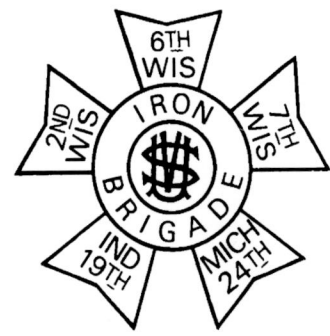

After the Maryland Campaign the Iron Brigade fell back towards Fredericksburg to make good their losses and reorganize, receiving while *en route* a new regiment, the Twenty-fourth Michigan which had been mustered on 29 July 1862. The Twenty-fourth were first issued with a uniform consisting of the typical *képi* and short dark blue blouse with light blue trousers. On 9 October while still in Maryland John Gibbon inspected them. The records say: 'We were drawn up in front of the rest of the Brigade whom we almost outnumbered. Our Colonel [Morrow] extolled our qualities, but the Brigade was silent. Not a cheer. A pretty cool reception, we thought.' The Michigan soldiers, however, were wrong in believing their new comrades hostile. The Iron Brigade as veterans were merely withholding full fellowship to the newcomers until they had shown themselves worthy of belonging to the Brigade.

At this period the depleted Second Wisconsin received one whole new company, and the Nineteenth Indiana some volunteer drafts, as also did the Sixth and Seventh Wisconsin.

On 30 October to the appropriate strains of 'Yankee Doodle' the Iron Brigade crossed pontoon bridges into Virginia, which State was described by one of the Michigan newcomers as the land of 'saucy secessionists where the young ladies sing secessionist songs'. Crossing Blue Ridge they reached Bloomfield where John Gibbon, on promotion, bade them farewell. This was a very sad day for him, he recalled later, because he was parting both from his 'gallant little brigade' and his own battery which had always accompanied it. Gibbon was replaced temporarily by Colonel Henry A. Morrow of the Twenty-fourth, who led the Brigade as far as Warrenton. There Colonel Cutler returned to duty recovered from his wound received at Brawner Farm, and with seniority over Morrow became commander until Solomon Meredith of the Nineteenth Indiana was promoted brigadier-general and took over permanently.

In November 1862, although conditions were becoming too wintry for operations to be easily conducted, a new Federal move against Richmond was planned, starting from Falmouth opposite Fredericksburg. Here the Rappahannock provided General Lee with a good defence line, and when a Federal attack seemed imminent he drew up his forces in a strong position on the hills to the west of the river.

Meanwhile, McClellan had been dismissed, and the Army of the Potomac turned over to his appointed successor General Ambrose Burnside. Without changing the corps structure, Burnside created three Grand Divisions of two corps each: Sumner's, which he ordered to attack opposite Fredericksburg; Franklin's – to which Doubleday's Division and the Iron Brigade belonged – which was to attack south of Fredericksburg; and Hooker's, which was held at first in reserve, but from which elements were sent later to the other two Grand Divisions.

Despite the weather the new campaign began well. By mid-November Sumner's Grand Division had reached the Rappahannock at Falmouth and the other two Grand Divisions were not far behind. The whole movement had been marked by rapid orderly marching in contrast to what Lincoln termed McClellan's 'slows' of the Peninsular and Maryland Campaigns. There was, however, a grave fault: bridging materials were not readily available. This meant that Lee was allowed ample time to prepare a really strong defensive position.

While the situation was developing in front of Fredericksburg, the Iron Brigade was put into camp with the rest of Franklin's I Corps at Aquia Creek. On 25 November they reached Brooks Station on the railroad between Aquia Creek and Fredericksburg. Here the Twenty-fourth Michigan were given the task of guarding the railroad, during which their companies were scattered over several miles of track, and they suffered a number of casualties from exposure to freezing winter rain. Meanwhile their comrades in the other regiments of the Brigade, having heard a rumour in camp that a cessation of hostilities had been agreed on for thirty days, proceeded hopefully to prepare themselves huts for the winter. However, on 9 December the order came for all of them to march away from Brooks Station downstream along the bank of the Rappahannock to cross with the rest of Franklin's men.

As they marched the sounds of battle could be clearly heard up north, and heavy clouds of smoke could be discerned rising above Fredericksburg; but they were not able to see how Sumner's troops were faring as thick woods separated them from the river's edge. After repeated halts the Brigade reached the river, but although the pontoon bridges had been made ready they were held back to let skirmishers go across and secure bridgeheads on the far side, and in the end they camped there for the night.

A heavy fog hung over the Rappahannock next morning. This hid them from the enemy but did not stop a hurricane of Confederate shells falling as they fell in at the call of their drums and bugles. VI Corps crossed first followed by I Corps led by the Iron Brigade's late commander John Gibbon's Division. Meade's Division followed, and Doubleday's with the Iron Brigade brought up the rear. Gibbon and Meade deployed their divisions at once, Gibbon to the right, joining up with elements of VI Corps, and Meade to the left. Doubleday, meanwhile, brought his artillery into action immediately after crossing to try to silence the Confederate guns, and then took his men downstream to Bernard House where, Battery B having been pulled in, the Iron Brigade spent the night. It was bitterly cold, and officers and men alike slept on the ground without fires, scraping together piles of leaves for bedding.

Franklin's crossing of the Rappahannock had been carried out without opposition except from artillery fire; but for Sumner's men in the north it was a different story. Owing to fierce musketry fire from skirmishers concealed in buildings on the outskirts of the town, the engineers could not set up the pontoons, and the advanced troops had

Lysander Cutler, Sixth Wisconsin

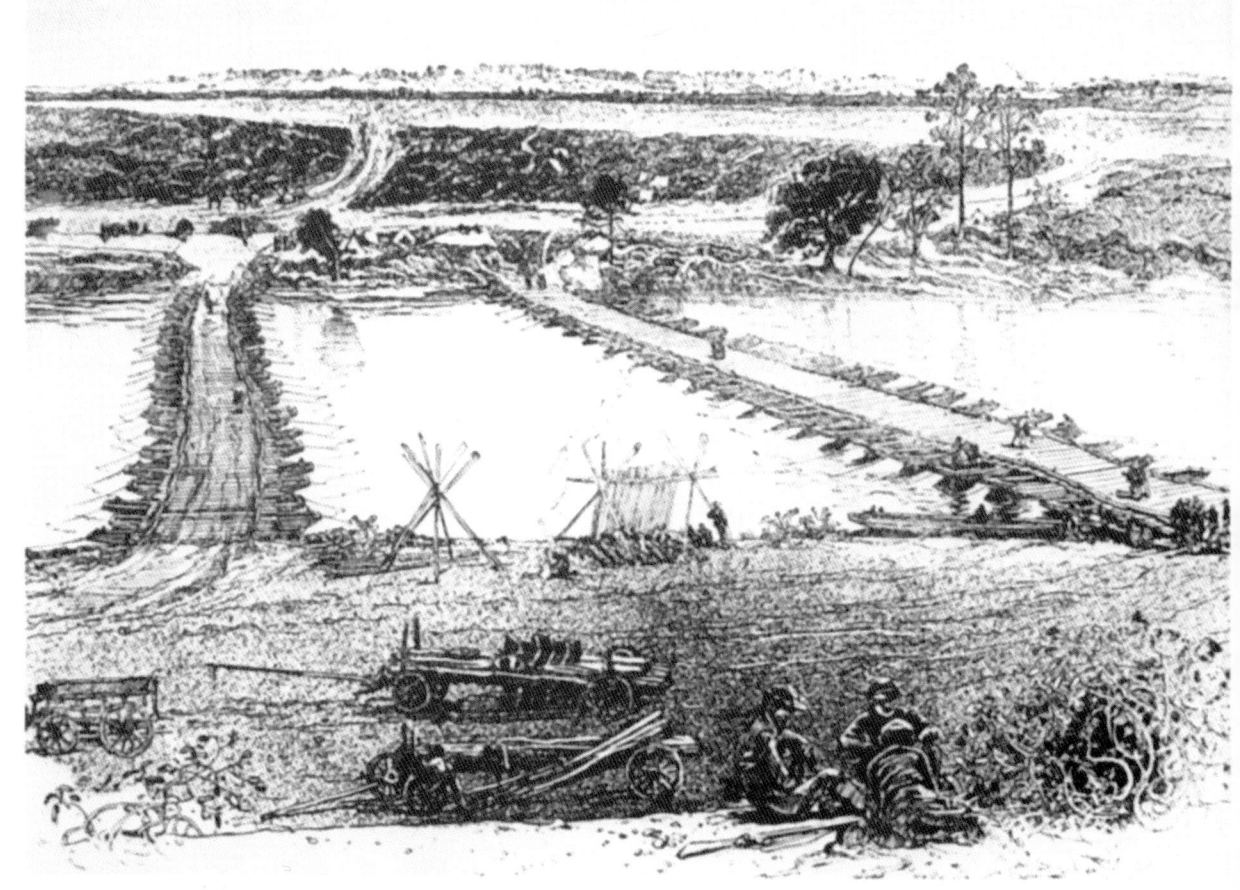

The pontoon bridges at Franklin's Crossing near Fredericksburg. The hills occupied by the Confederates can be seen in the distance

eventually to cross in pontoon boats. Nor did the assault meet with any success when it was eventually staged, for murderous fire from Marye's Hill and the sunken road at its base decimated Sumner's men and the elements from Hooker's Grand Division who joined them.

Before this, on 13 December, Burnside had ordered Franklin to attack; and Meade's Division was sent forward against Jackson's Corps on the south of the Confederate line, with Gibson's Division on Meade's right and Doubleday's to his left rear.

Meade, starting from near the wood by Smithfield Farm, had to cross Bowling Green Road and the railroad to reach Jackson's position among the wooded hills to the west – see map 4. As his dark blue columns crossed the road enemy shells fell among them, so Federal artillery was brought into action between the road and railway for counter-battery work. When Meade's men began their assault on Jackson's position between the headwaters of a stream, Doubleday moved his force down-river to protect Meade's flank as best he could.

In four lines of battle, with the Iron Brigade and Battery B in front nearest the river, the Division advanced towards Smithfield Wood, facing as it did so a strong line of Confederate cavalry interspersed with horse artillery, led by General Jeb Stuart with Major Pelham in charge of the guns. After the wood had been shelled by Battery B and skirmishers from the U.S. Sharpshooters sent forward, the Iron Brigade was ordered to clear it of enemy, and the Twenty-fourth Michigan and Seventh Wisconsin were placed in the lead for the task.

At the end of the wood the Twenty-fourth passed through the Sharpshooters and, clambering

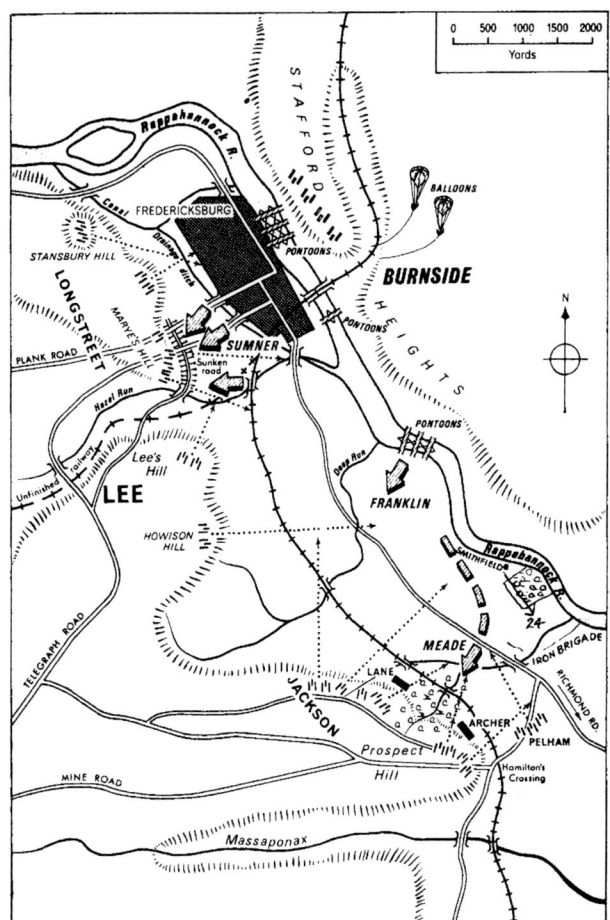

4 The Battle of Fredericksburg, 13 December 1862

ploughed through their ranks, taking off the arm of one soldier and the head of another. As they were becoming unsettled, Colonel Morrow immediately took them in hand. Pulling them back under cover he gave them a period of arms drill as if they were on parade. When they were more composed he led them forward again, and as a shell fell nearby, he steeled them with the cry of, 'Steady now, those Wisconsin men are watching you.' Then, although they still suffered casualties as they moved forward, they neutralized the artillery piece by putting its detachment to flight and drove back its supporting skirmishers.

It was now early afternoon, and Meade's men having initially pierced Jackson's line were in the process of being hurled back by Jackson's reserves.

over the fence, swept on through the trees in great style carrying the wood and capturing a number of prisoners and horses, a feat which earned the new regiment deserved praise from the Divisional Commander in his report. Continuing its advance beyond the wood in the wake of the Twenty-fourth the rest of the Iron Brigade established a defence line to secure Meade's flank. This they held successfully for the rest of the operation.

Battery B came into action near this new defence line to try and silence enemy guns which were harassing the infantry they were supporting. Out in the open the men and horses of the battery began to go down under the fire from a Federal battery ahead, so the Twenty-fourth Michigan were sent forward to silence the guns and sharp-shooters nearby who were menacing Battery B. The Twenty-fourth rose up and advanced, but as they did so were met with a hail of shot which

Solomon Meredith, Nineteenth Indiana, the third and last Commander of the Iron Brigade

As Confederate guns were still firing a furious cannonade, the men of the Iron Brigade sought protection by lying flat in ditches or hugging the ground. The Federal artillery, however, still stayed in action, and Battery B particularly distinguished itself under the leadership of Lieutenant Stewart. On one occasion an enemy caisson was seen to be struck and knocked to pieces by one of its shells, and some of the enemy crew flung into the air.

By the time darkness fell, the Federal line, although drawn back in places, was still firmly held; and the Confederates were confining themselves to long-range musketry fire and artillery fire, not making any attempt to break through.

Although both Franklin's and Sumner's Grand Divisions had been decisively defeated in the battle, General Burnside continued to occupy the enemy side of the river throughout next day while deciding whether or not to renew the assault. At first there was artillery and picket fire from both sides, but this was soon interspersed with periods of informal truce during which the two sides mingled freely, buried their dead and succoured their wounded.

There was quiet on the Iron Brigade's front on the night of 14 December 1862 because of a truce arranged so that both sides could get some rest. This was broken for a brief spell when reliefs not informed of the arrangement opened fire in error. Early next day, still in a period of truce, a fist fight was arranged near the Bowling Green Road between a Confederate and a Sixth Wisconsin soldier. Both sides watched while the combatants took part in what was eventually declared to everyone's satisfaction a drawn fight. There were then handshakes all round and tobacco and coffee were traded.

On 15 December the Iron Brigade carried out two short reconnaissances downstream, and when they returned were told that a general withdrawal had been decided on. Although the risk of detection was lessened by a favourable wind blowing from the Confederate line, there was still doubt as to whether Burnside's men could get back across the river unscathed. The artillery was sent back first. Battery B was in an exposed position near the Confederate picket line without much infantry support, so the guns were left shotted with

Colonel Morrow who commanded the Twenty-fourth Michigan at Fredericksburg, where this last regiment to join the Iron Brigade distinguished itself (Burton Historical Collection)

canister and primed for action to deal with any enemy rush, and limbered up and drawn away as silently as possible. Once all the artillery had crossed the river it was the infantry's turn. Rather than disclose the withdrawal it was at first decided to sacrifice the pickets, which for the Iron Brigade meant leaving behind the Nineteenth Indiana after the pontoon bridges were broken up. In the end, Colonel Cutler, who was in charge of the withdrawal, persuaded the Corps Commander to let him bring them back if he could. At 4.30 a.m., therefore, the pickets were called in and told to move back to the river, and to be both quick and silent if they wanted to save themselves. The Nineteenth Indiana were the only troops left facing Jackson's Corps, and in their retreat to the pontoons were pursued by Confederate cavalry. Without any panic they fell back, and all but the rearguard crossed over safely. For the rearguard it was a near thing. Before they reached the water's edge the engineers, feeling they could no longer risk a Confederate assault on the bridge, broke up the pontoons and sent them drifting downstream. They left a few skiffs for the rearguard. Fortunately these proved sufficient. With the enemy cavalry close on their heels they escaped in them to the safety of the northern bank, and not a single soldier of the Nineteenth Indiana was captured.

Back on the north side of the river the Iron Brigade went into camp two miles from Franklin's Crossing. The campaign of Fredericksburg was over. Although the Federal Army had suffered fearful casualties, particularly Sumner's Corps in the north while assaulting Marye's Hill, the Iron Brigade had suffered less severely than most, and at the same time Battery B had won more renown and the Twenty-fourth Michigan established their reputation. Only 65 Westerners were casualties, 32 from the Twenty-fourth Michigan, and B Battery lost 8 men and 11 horses. Lieutenant Stewart and the Battery earned the praise of the Army, and General Solomon Meredith in his report stated that the Twenty-fourth showed themselves worthy of association with the old Iron Brigade, a verdict which the Wisconsin and Indiana men fully endorsed. They had watched their untried comrades, and now considered that they had earned the right to full membership of the Iron Brigade – and their black hats if available.

Chancellorsville

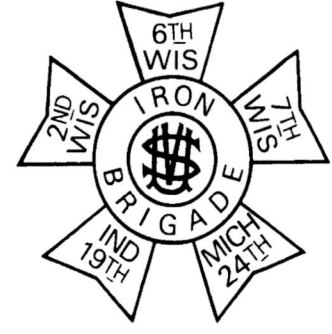

After Fredericksburg the Iron Brigade marched through the mud to nearby Belle Plain and went into winter quarters until April 1863 when they were alerted to take part in the Chancellorsville Campaign.

The new commander who replaced the discredited Burnside was General 'Fighting Joe' Hooker. Hooker did away with Burnside's Grand Divisions and substituted a single corps organization again. He was soon very pleased with his reorganized army, and even more sanguine about the plans he evolved to crush Lee's forces around Fredericksburg and march on Richmond. 'My plans are perfect,' he exclaimed. 'May God have mercy on General Lee, for I will have none.'

Hooker's plan consisted of a giant pincer movement. As a preliminary feint, Sedgwick's forces,

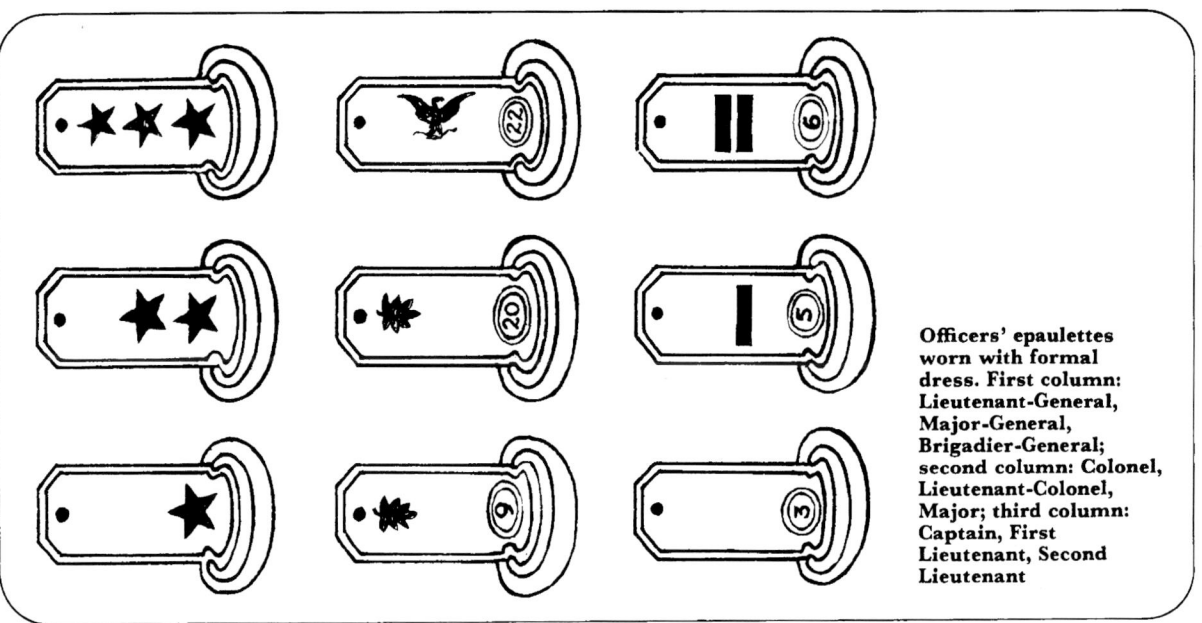

Officers' epaulettes worn with formal dress. First column: Lieutenant-General, Major-General, Brigadier-General; second column: Colonel, Lieutenant-Colonel, Major; third column: Captain, First Lieutenant, Second Lieutenant

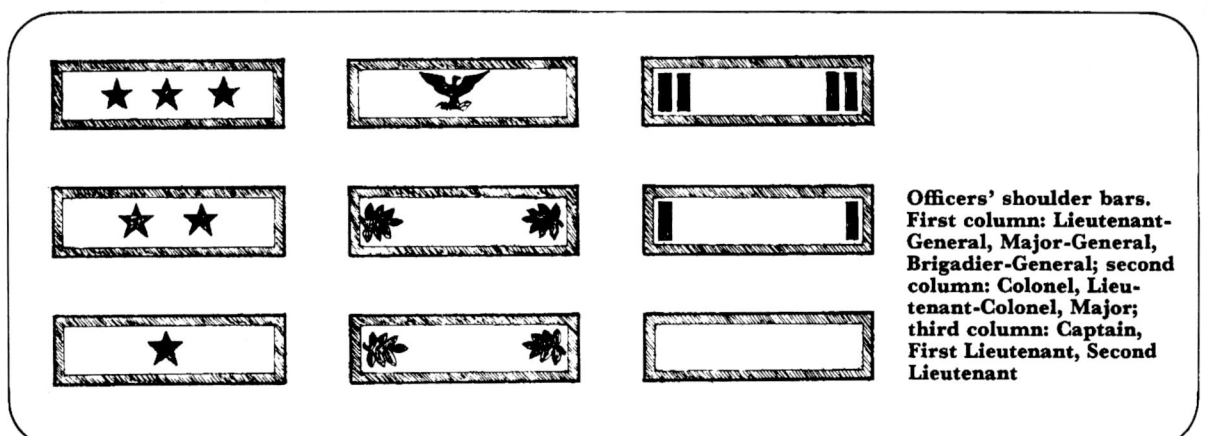

Officers' shoulder bars. First column: Lieutenant-General, Major-General, Brigadier-General; second column: Colonel, Lieutenant-Colonel, Major; third column: Captain, First Lieutenant, Second Lieutenant

which included Reynolds's I Corps and the Iron Brigade, were to cross the Rappahannock below Fredericksburg; then Hooker would march the rest of his army westwards up-river. Coming back across the Rappahannock and Rapidan well to the north-west, he would march his men through the Wilderness and attack the Confederate position at Fredericksburg from the rear while Sedgwick was assaulting it frontally. Meanwhile, the Cavalry Corps under General Stoneham was to sweep far to the west round Lee's flank and cut his communications with Richmond.

As part of Sedgwick's operations, a masking diversion was carried out below Fredericksburg in which two corps crossed the Rappahannock on pontoon bridges at Franklin's old crossing-point and four miles downstream opposite Smithfield Wood which also had featured in the December 1862 fight. The Iron Brigade was in General Wadsworth's 1st Division of General Reynolds's I Corps, one of the corps involved. Consequently they set off down the left bank of the Rappahannock again. They passed White Oak Church and halted in the grounds of Fitzhugh House, a mansion of some pretentions but ravaged by the war and very dilapidated. While the Western soldiers rested or investigated casually the abandoned house, their officers worked out a plan for the crossing. The river at Fitzhugh's was about 200 yards wide with steep banks, and the far side was covered with undergrowth among which the Confederates had constructed rifle-pits and field fortifications. It was deemed necessary to neutralize these commanding enemy works so that the engineers could set up the pontoons and build the bridges, and the Iron Brigade was selected to dash across during the night and seize the enemy strongpoints.

Following a meeting of the regimental commanders at General Solomon Meredith's headquarters when the plan was detailed, the Iron Brigade advanced as quickly as possible to the river's edge. All was quiet, but the boats were not there. The men stood by under arms, waiting, but the boats did not arrive. The hour of the assault passed and still the boats did not come. Slowly the time ran out and finally the day dawned. It was too late now to make the crossing, although in the end the boats did appear. Taking a chance the engineers were set to work on constructing the bridges regardless of the enemy on the opposite bank; but they were soon under fire. At a range of 200 yards the Confederates could hardly miss, and their shots not only took a heavy toll of the engineers, but stampeded the mules and brought down the pontoon wagons. On this, the engineers were recalled from the water's edge, and the Twenty-fourth Michigan, the Sixth Wisconsin and Fourteenth Brooklyn were sent down in their place to engage the enemy. Partially protected by a stone wall that ran down to the bank at an angle, they opened fire. The morning fog was now slowly lifting so the Confederate works became visible, but their fire on them did not seem to have as much effect as the Confederate return fire was having.

General Reynolds now realized that drastic measures would be required if the crossing was to be made safe. His new plan was an adaptation of the night operation. The Twenty-fourth Michigan and Sixth Wisconsin were to make the crossing in pontoon boats, like Sumner's men at Fredericksburg, assisted by the Second Wisconsin whose task was to run down the position wagons and launch the boats. The remaining regiments of the Iron Brigade with the Fourteenth Brooklyn were to give covering fire from the edge of the river, and then follow across.

One company was assigned to each boat which had four oarsmen, and they were told to lie down as they crossed. When the order to advance was given, the Westerners ran down to the bank and leaped into the boats. Immediately there was a roar of fire from both sides, and bullets whizzed into the boats killing and maiming some of the prone figures sheltering behind the all-too-flimsy gunwales. But the casualties were not confined to one side. As the boats touched the far shore some of the enemy standing on the bank and clearly defined were seen to roll down into the water, victims of the Federal covering fire. The Federals jumped into the mud and water, waist deep, and waded ashore. There they crawled or scrambled up the bank, clutching at bushes to help them on their way. Bayonets fixed, the Sixth Wisconsin and Twenty-fourth Michigan charged the Confederate fortifications; but very few shots were exchanged or casualties received before the enemy took to flight. Both the Sixth and Twenty-fourth were later to claim that they were the first to climb out of the river-bed and reach the top of the bank. It is difficult to decide, for they were neck and neck; but anyhow the result was a grand victory. The Twenty-fourth had 21 casualties in the whole operation, the Sixth had 16, and the other regiments of the Iron Brigade which were giving covering fire from the north bank had 20 between them. For these losses 90 prisoners were taken as well as guns from the abandoned redoubts.

When the Iron Brigade had established a bridgehead on the south bank, the bridging of the river began. It did not take long now for the pontoons to be put into position, and the track laid, and so the 1st Division was soon able to cross. It looked for a time as if General Wadsworth's men having reinforced the bridgehead would have to fight a full-scale battle, for shortly after the bridges were completed, the Confederates reappeared in force, and having manned the entrenchments on the wooded hills of the December fight, sent skirmishers across the railroad and Bowling Green Road towards Smithfield Wood. The enemy's main force, however, did not advance from the hills, and soon the soldiers had worked out one of their informal picket-line truces, permitting both sides a restful night. Since an extended truce could not be depended on, the Federals spent the next day digging in and throwing up breastworks reinforced with ploughs and reapers from the nearby farm. Late in the day the enemy artillery opened up again and a solid shot killed or wounded four men of the Twenty-fourth Michigan. On this, Battery B was fetched across the river to engage in counter-battery work.

By this time Hooker's envelopment was developing. His corps had surmounted the obstacle of the two rivers, and were moving through the Wilderness towards the rear of the Confederate position at Fredericksburg – see map 4.

Early on 2 May Reynolds's Corps was ordered to recross the Rappahannock and march up the left bank to reinforce Hooker's enveloping army.

Union N.C.O.s' sleeve chevrons. Top row: Corporal, Sergeant, First Sergeant; bottom row: Ordnance Sergeant, Quartermaster Sergeant, Sergeant-Major. The colour of the chevrons was light blue on a dark blue coat

The Confederates soon realized what was happening. They opened fire on Reynolds's men, and one shell hit the bridge and damaged a boat. Repairs having been made, the men crawled from their temporary fortifications and headed for the river. As before the Iron Brigade was the last to leave, and this time it was the pickets of the Twenty-fourth Michigan who were not able to cross until the bridges were withdrawn, and had to make the passage by boat. Leaving two companies of the Seventh Wisconsin to cover the engineers loading the pontoons, General Wadsworth formed up his division and began the march north.

While the Iron Brigade was marching north, Hooker passed through the Wilderness and emerging on its eastern fringe by Chancellor House, encountered the Confederate troops sent from Fredericksburg to halt his advance. On this, Hooker drew back his men into the forest, and put them into defensive positions around Chancellor House and south of the turnpike past Wilderness Church towards Wilderness Tavern.

Lee and Jackson, who were both now present opposite Hooker, conferred among the pines near the crossroads south-east of Chancellor House, after which Jackson was sent on his famous march round Hooker's west flank. Jackson caught the men of Howard's XI Corps completely unawares, and drove them back in confusion on Chancellor House. As darkness fell Jackson was mortally wounded by his own men; but the result of the daring manœuvre was to hem in Hooker's forces around Chancellor House, and weaken Hooker's will to continue the fight.

By the time the Confederate assault had been halted, Reynolds's Corps, including the Iron Brigade, having completed its 20-mile march from Fredericksburg, arrived at the field of battle, and was directed to extend the west flank of the Federal forces round Chancellor House so as to continue the line to the Rapidan.

With his line reorganized and reinforced, Hooker stood on the defensive; but he was not able to resist the new Confederate attacks, and gradually his men were driven northwards towards United States Ford. A lucky shell from a Confederate gun may have helped to decide the battle. Hooker was standing on the balcony of Chancellor House when one of the pillars supporting the balcony above was hit, and a fragment struck him on the head. He was dazed and concussed. He managed to mount a horse and ride a mile to the north where he found a soldier's tent and stretched himself down; but he was very confused and the will to continue the fight had left him. He could no longer grasp that with Sedgwick in Lee's rear a strong thrust could win the battle. He decided to leave Sedgwick to his fate. He handed over command to General Couch and told him to withdraw to the other side of the river. Meanwhile Lee realized that Hooker at Chancellor House posed no real threat any longer and turned on Sedgwick and drove him over the river.

In their entrenchments beyond Chancellor House the Iron Brigade heard rumours of all these happenings. After an uncomfortable night in the open when, as was the custom of the Brigade, officers and men slept on the ground without blankets, the Twenty-fourth Michigan was sent on 4 May on picket duty to Ely's Ford on the Rapidan, and the remainder spent an uneventful day. It was the same on 5 May. As darkness fell on the second night, however, the beginnings of the Federal withdrawal became apparent, for

General Reynolds with officers

1 Infantryman, Second Wisconsin, 1861;
2 Infantryman, Nineteenth Indiana, 1861;
3 Infantryman, Sixth Wisconsin, 1861

1 Drummer, Rufus King's Brigade, 1861;
2 Infantryman, Rufus King's Brigade, 1861;
3 N.C.O., Rufus King's Brigade, 1861

1 Infantryman, General Gibbon's Brigade, 1862;
2 Infantryman, General Gibbon's Brigade, 1862;
3 Senior Officer, General Gibbon's Brigade, 1862

1 N.C.O., Iron Brigade, 1863;
2 Junior Officer, Iron Brigade, 1863-4;
3 Infantryman, Iron Brigade, 1862-3

1 N.C.O., Hall's Battery, 1863;
2 Infantryman, Iron Brigade, 1863-4;
3 Artilleryman, Battery B, 1861-5

Artillery Officer, Battery B, 1861-5

Mounted Officer, Iron Brigade, 1861-5

G

Officer, Buford's Cavalry, 1863

of the Potomac moved eastwards in the direction of Fredericksburg. The rain continued to fall, and 100,000 miserable and discouraged men waded through the mud and made their way towards Falmouth. Here 15 miles from United States Ford the Brigade encamped. On 7 May the Westerners marched on with I Corps past White Oak Church to Fitzhugh House where they reoccupied their camp of 28 April. The campaign of Chancellorsville was now over, and they were back where they started from.

Gettysburg

The men of the Iron Brigade were fortunate in their quarters at Fitzhugh House, with water handy and 'a surround of beautiful trees'. Having set up camp the Westerners settled down to the routine of regular drill and picket duty with added comforts from an illicit trade with the enemy for which they constructed miniature boats to sail coffee across the Rappahannock in exchange for Southern tobacco.

Camp life allowed them time to think and talk about the rumours that were always running through the Army, one of which suggested that Lee was planning to invade the North to attack Washington and Baltimore.

As May 1863 drew to a close amidst the continuing gossip about a Confederate thrust into Maryland and Pennsylvania, the Twenty-fourth Michigan at last received their coveted black hats, earned almost six months previously at Fredericksburg, but at least received in time to wear at a parade for their State Governor and his wife then visiting the Army. There followed a period of

John B. Callis, Seventh Wisconsin (State Historical Society of Wisconsin)

mules were ordered to be loaded up and sent to the rear along with other baggage. At 3.30 a.m. on 6 May in a drizzling rain I Corps began its movement towards United States Ford on the Rappahannock, the Iron Brigade bringing up the rear. At 5.00 a.m. the river was reached, and the pontoon bridges being choked, the troops of 1st Division occupied a rearguard position to cover the crossing. After waiting three hours, they crossed themselves. Once across the river the Army

25

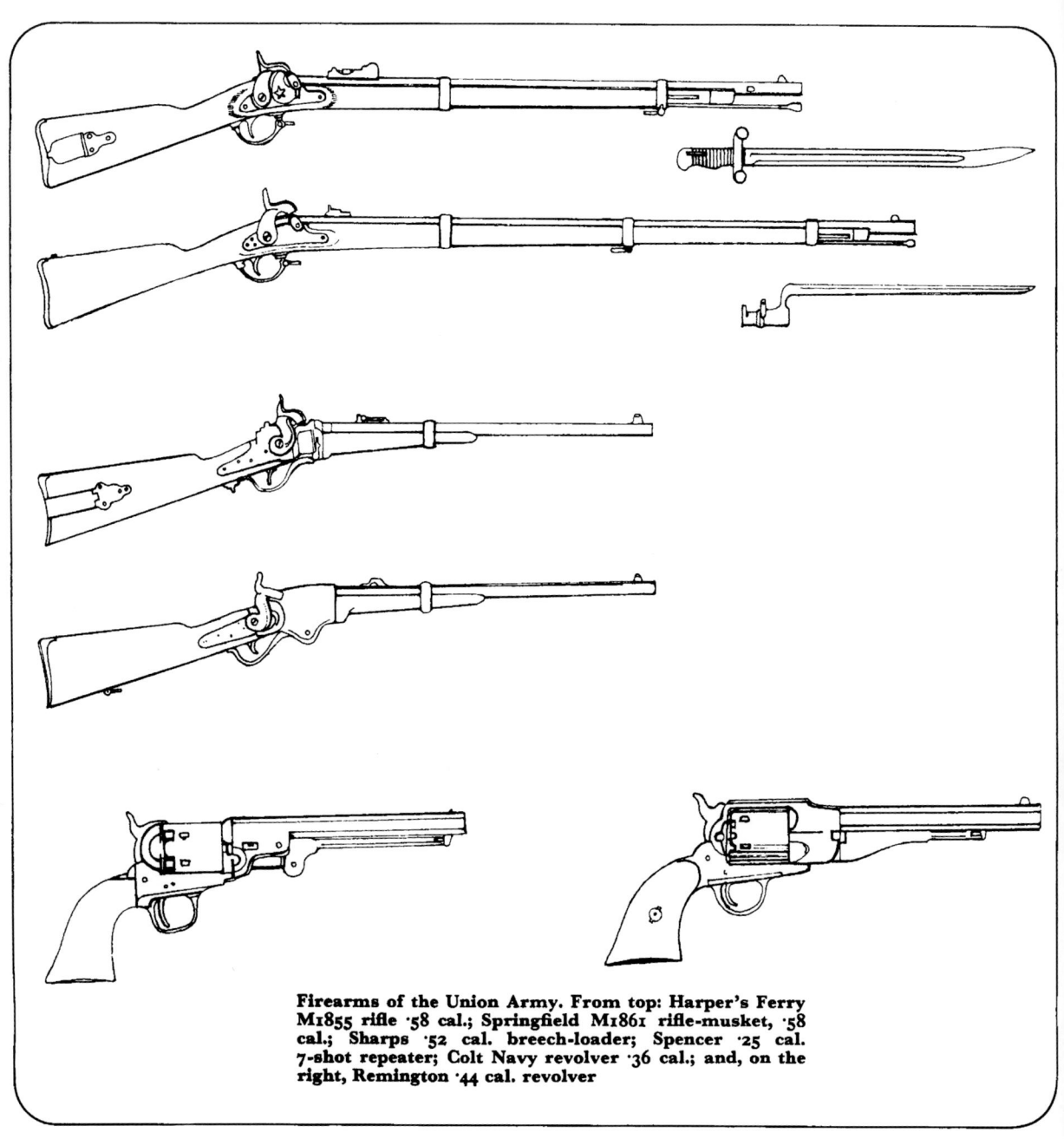

Firearms of the Union Army. From top: Harper's Ferry M1855 rifle ·58 cal.; Springfield M1861 rifle-musket, ·58 cal.; Sharps ·52 cal. breech-loader; Spencer ·25 cal. 7-shot repeater; Colt Navy revolver ·36 cal.; and, on the right, Remington ·44 cal. revolver

reorganization and reduction when several regiments which had been enlisted for only two years were disbanded. This meant a reduction of 5,000 in General Wadsworth's 1st Division, and two brigades instead of four. The Iron Brigade under General Solomon Meredith, however, remained intact, and by the rearrangement had the distinction of becoming the First Brigade of the First Division of the First Corps of the Army, custodians, too, of the flag of the First Division, 'a large white triangle with a red sphere in the center'.

In June 1863 the rumoured advance of General Lee's armies into Maryland and Pennsylvania became fact; and, General Hooker having resigned and been replaced by General Meade, the Army of the Potomac were to take the road north again, this time with the Iron Brigade in the van.

On 4 June the Federals began to notice that the Confederates were moving away; but there was continuing uncertainty as to their destination. The Iron Brigade like the rest of the Army of the Potomac was put into a state of readiness; but it was not until 12 June that they got under way, and began a long and gruelling march – it always seemed to be too wet or too hot – towards Manassas Junction and the north. They passed the scene of their former engagements at Brawner Farm and Bull Run, and proceeded into a camp near Centreville, the men 'tired, sore, sleepy, hungry, dusty, and dirty as pigs'.

Lee's Army had by this time crossed the Potomac and moved north through the Antietam area into Pennsylvania and seemed to be making as if to threaten Baltimore. At the end of June it was reported to be at Chambersburg and moving east to seek a store of shoes in the little town of Gettysburg.

In high spirits I Corps moved north parallel to Lee's Army, but further to the east, and approached Gettysburg from the south-east just as the Confederate van were moving east to occupy the town. General Meade gave order to General Reynolds to move into Gettysburg and Wadsworth's division with Buford's cavalry and the Iron Brigade in front took the road for the town. Colonel Rufus Dawes placed the drums and fifes at the head of the Sixth Wisconsin and had the colors unfurled. Then to the tune of 'The Campbells Are Coming' they swung up the road with the intention of making a show before the people of Gettysburg. As they approached the town, firing was heard ahead. It was Buford's troopers brushing with the van of the Confederates west of the town. After an hour's skirmishing the cavalry fell back and had just occupied McPherson's Ridge, and Seminary Ridge behind, when up rode General Reynolds on reconnaissance ahead of his division. Reynolds and Buford ascended to the cupola of the Seminary building to view the country and saw the long grey columns of Confederate infantry moving down the Chambersburg Turnpike beside the unfinished railway cutting towards them. Despite the fact that the enemy appeared to have a superiority in numbers, Reynolds decided to fight. Dispatching a rider to tell General Meade of the situation, he rode back to hasten his men along.

The Iron Brigade and Cutler's Brigade were the first into action. The Twenty-fourth Wisconsin and Nineteenth Indiana advanced on McPherson's Ridge to the west, the Seventh Wisconsin and Second Wisconsin made for McPherson's Woods, and Cutler's regiments advanced up between the pike and the railroad cutting, and beyond the cutting. They were soon all in head-on collision with the enemy. It is recorded by an eye-witness from the Second that on their front 'a line of ragged dirty blue crashed into one of dirty, ragged butternut'. At a range of 40 yards the first Confederate volley opened telling gaps in the Wisconsin line, but as at Brawner Farm the Wisconsins plunged forward, pouring a hot fire into the enemy. When the Seventh reached the crest of McPherson's Ridge they checked until the Nineteenth Indiana and Twenty-fourth Michigan on their left caught up and extended the line to their left. Then they all surged forward again and

General Meade who commanded the Federal forces at Gettysburg

Hollon Richardson, Seventh Wisconsin (State Historical Society of Wisconsin)

William W. Dudley, Nineteenth Indiana (State Historical Society of Wisconsin)

swept the Confederate soldiers over Willoughby Run and back into the woods beyond.

Elsewhere however, things had not gone so well. General Reynolds had dropped dead, victim of a sharpshooter's bullet, and three of Cutler's regiments on the right were thrown back in confusion to Seminary Ridge. This exposed the regiments and the Maine Battery between the cutting and the pike, and they fell back in sympathy. The situation was restored, however, by Colonel Rufus Dawes and the reserve drawn from all the Iron Brigade regiments. He led them across to the right at the double-quick and struck the wheeling grey line just as it was threatening the Westerners on the ridge. Dawes's horse was struck and he fell to the ground; but he was not hurt, and his men gave him a cheer as he dashed forward to lead them on foot. The regiments retreating between the pike and cutting now checked and joined up with Dawes's men. Together they stormed the railroad cutting, and moved up in it, taking the Confederates in enfilade. Temporarily overwhelmed, the Confederates started to surrender, and Dawes eventually drew back with 230 prisoners, including 7 officers, and a gun left by the Maine Battery when they had to fall back earlier on Seminary Ridge. Hurled back everywhere, the Confederates now withdrew across Willoughby Run, and the first phase of the battle west of Gettysburg had been won, and by the Federals.

There was a lull of more than two hours before the battle was joined again by which time General Howard, XI Corps, and part of I Corps, had arrived in Gettysburg, and Howard had taken over command of the forward troops. Howard ordered them to hold their positions on McPherson's Ridge, and placed elements of the rest of his force on the north part of Seminary Ridge and on Cemetery Hill, thus creating three defence lines in the path of the advancing Confederate Army.

At 3.00 p.m., heralded by artillery fire, the Confederates attacked again. When they approached Willoughby Run the Iron Brigade poured a converging fire on them so that, for a time, 'no rebel crossed the stream alive'. Solomon Meredith became a casualty at this stage, crushed beneath his horse. The front remained impregnable, but again the flanks began to yield. When the regiments on the left pulled back, they exposed to enfilade fire the Nineteenth Indiana; and when the right went, the other Iron Brigade regiments found they were being fired on from their right rear. To obviate this the Westerners concentrated in the south-east corner of McPherson's Woods, and then, when that did not suffice, pulled back to a barricade of rails on Seminary Ridge.

From behind this feeble barricade, supported by the Maine Battery, they stemmed the fierce tide which pressed upon them incessantly, and held back the enemy lines. Meanwhile, north of the pike on the right, B Battery and the Sixth Wisconsin were resisting just as fiercely. Thus the Brigade held the line on either side of the Chambersburg pike until the other troops had withdrawn to Cemetery Hill. Then again outflanked on both right and left they could stay no longer. First the batteries, then the regiments retreated, the Seventh and Sixth being the last, and finally they fell back themselves to Cemetery Hill and Culps Hill to play a reduced part in the last phases of the Battle of Gettysburg.

With 1,200 casualties out of a total of 1,800 who entered the battle their losses had been indeed grievous; but by holding off the Confederates on the west of the town they enabled the rest of Meade's army to place themselves in strong defensive positions south of the town on Culps Hill, Cemetery Hill and Cemetery Ridge. Despite fierce attacks by Ewell's men in the north, by Longstreet's and Hood's in the south, and Pickett's famous charge on the centre of the Federal line, the Confederate Army was unable to dislodge them. Thus the gallant Iron Brigade played an important part in deciding the outcome of the battle, and in the final triumph of the North.

The Maine Battery in action between the Cutting and the Chambersburg Turnpike at Gettysburg

Gettysburg may be classed as their last stand. After the battle their huge losses were made up with men from many States of the Union, and although they played a valuable part under General Grant in the final advance on Richmond, this new unit could no longer be reckoned as the old Iron Brigade of Westerners.

The Last Period

The Battle of Gettysburg had been won, but the war was far from ended; and when on 13 June 1863 the Confederates crossed the Potomac, the Union Army, including the remnants of the Iron Brigade, followed them to Virginia to fight on for two more years. The march south had hardly begun when a new regiment joined. There was a good reason for this as the Brigade was down to 800 men; but the choice could not have been a worse one. From VII Corps came the 167th Pennsylvania, nine-month draftees whose term was about to expire. It was bad enough to receive Easterners; in addition the Pennsylvanians were so badly disciplined that mutiny was one of their first acts of membership. With the complicity of their officers who were conscripts elected by the men, the Regiment refused to march on the grounds that their enlistments had expired. The rest of the Brigade were promptly placed under arms, and the orders 'Ready' and 'Aim' had actually been given before their new comrades changed their minds. After this the Sixth Wisconsin were placed behind them on the line of march with instructions to shoot any man who fell out. This instruction the Sixth's Colonel, Rufus Dawes, interpreted as meaning that they should drive them when they lagged; so that from then on the proud Westerners referred to the 167th as 'the cattle'. Fortunately the association was shortlived, for a month later, when their term officially expired, they were mustered out and replaced by a battalion of the New York Sharpshooters. In addition, there came as recruits individual groups of volunteers and draftees, initially also scorned and labelled 'hounds', but who came to fight courageously alongside the Brigade's veterans in the closing stages of the war. Among these were 14 Indians, assigned to the Seventh Wisconsin. They could not speak English, but were adept at camouflage, being said to have 'covered their bodies very ingeniously with boughs of pine to conceal themselves in the woods, and to have added a genuine war whoop on the appropriate occasion'. Whatever the merits, however, of those joining after Gettysburg, the replacements were largely a different type from the earlier enthusiastic and eager volunteers who gained the Iron Brigade its reputation.

A little of this reputation still lingered on during the last two years of the war when the Brigade was but a ghost of its old self. Because of the Iron Brigade's past accomplishments, an enterprising music publisher brought out an "Iron Brigade Quickstep'; also a special Iron Brigade flag was commissioned by citizens from Wisconsin, Indiana and Michigan living in Washington.

After Gettysburg new faces among the enlisted men were matched by new faces among the officers. During the early part of the period the Commander of the Iron Brigade was Lysander Cutler

On Seminary Ridge on the first day of Gettysburg, by the cupola from which Buford and Reynolds viewed the field of battle

General Reynolds, the Iron Brigade's Divisional Commander at Gettysburg

who replaced Solomon Meredith. On 20 October 1863 the Second Wisconsin lost Colonel Lucius Fairchild, permanently disabled by the loss of an arm. For a time Colonel Rufus Dawes commanded the Sixth Wisconsin, but he left the army on 5 July 1864 before the end of hostilities. The oldest surviving regimental commander, Colonel Morrow, was wounded at Petersburg and left the Iron Brigade.

The period after Gettysburg saw the introduction of the 'Veteran System'. This endeavoured to induce old soldiers due to be mustered out to volunteer for an additional term of three years or the duration of the war. The Twenty-fourth Michigan were not due to muster out until 1865, but the other regiments were supposed to go in the spring and summer of 1864. After their regimental officers had presented soberly the terms offered for re-enlistment, which included a thirty-day furlough before continuing, the men were subjected to a good deal of pressurization by officials in

Battery B, Fourth United States Artillery. It was formed in 1821, and fought with distinction in the Florida War of 1837 and the Mexican War of 1845. In October 1861 it was permanently attached to the Iron Brigade. Here it is in action at Gettysburg under Lieutenant Stewart

Washington anxious to rebuild the Army. The result was that three-quarters of the men of the old regiments of the Iron Brigade agreed to serve on. When Rufus Dawes proudly presented the result for his Sixth Wisconsin he said: 'Our detached men who have been cooks for officers, hostlers, clerks and teamsters of whom there are sixty-eight, nearly all decline to re-enlist, but the men who have stood by the old flag through fair and foul weather, and through many bloody battles, almost to a man dedicate their lives and service anew to their country.'

In March 1864, after a long winter in defence positions along the Rappahannock, General Grant, who had been brought from the west after his victories at Vicksburg and Chattanooga, announced the start of the final campaign in the east to capture Richmond and end the war. Before operations began the Iron Brigade had a meeting with Grant which Colonel Rufus Dawes described as follows:

'The troops were drawn up in line of battalions *en masse* doubled on the center. There was a cold drizzle of rain and as General Grant at the head of his staff and escort rode slowly along in front of the line, regiment after regiment gave loud cheers in his honor as he approached. This had become customary in our army when the troops were reviewed by the commanding general. General Grant made no recognition of the intended compliment. I was in command of the regiment, and, observing this, felt provoked. I turned to the regiment and said: "As General Grant does not seem to think our cheering worth notice, I will not call for cheers. Maintain your position as soldiers." When General Grant came to the Sixth Wisconsin, the military salutes required were performed with exact precision and the men stood motionless as statues. He evidently expected them to cheer him as the others had; but when he saw us performing only our exact and formal duties as soldiers, he took

Thomas S. Allen, Second Wisconsin (Library of Congress)

off his hat and made a low bow to us, and to our colors dipped in salute to him as commander of the army.'

The men of the Iron Brigade were very pleased about this, and remarked among themselves that 'Grant wants soldiers, not yaupers'.

Before the coming campaigns there was a considerable amount of reorganization of the Army of the Potomac. General Meade's force was consolidated into three corps, and among corps eliminated was the old I Corps which was absorbed in General G. K. Warren's V Corps. This caused a good deal of dissatisfaction among the members of the Iron Brigade, one of whom remarked, 'the Brigade . . . would lose their identity purchased with blood and held most sacred'. The chagrin at the destruction of I Corps was salved to some extent by an order permitting the men to wear their old corps badges. In spite of the reorganization there were many well-known faces about. The command of the 4th Division, to which the Iron Brigade was allotted, went to General James S. Wadsworth, at last returned to duty, and Lysander Cutler assumed command of the Iron Brigade which included the five old regiments, the now familiar New York Sharpshooters, and the Seventh Indiana. Wadsworth's artillery also included the brass guns of 'Bloody B', as the soldiers of the Iron Brigade called their favourite battery. Many of the battery's Western soldiers had returned to their regiments – a process that was to be accelerated as the war continued – and only 57 men from the original Iron Brigade remained with the guns; but Lieutenant Stewart was still the artillery commander, and the affinity between Battery B and the Brigade was to continue.

Grant evolved a great design to assail Virginia from all sides. His most trusted subordinate Sherman was left in the West with the task of driving through Georgia to the east coast and then moving north on Richmond. General Sigel was set in motion down the Shenandoah Valley to cut Confederate links with the west at Lynchburg. General Butler was dispatched with his army to move up the James River on Petersburg and Richmond from the east. Meanwhile General Meade's army, with which the Iron Brigade served, was to advance on Richmond from the north. Then, within the pattern of this convergent attack on General Lee's armies, a major pincer movement was to come into action between the two major elements of the Federal forces, Meade's army coming down from the north and Sherman's army moving up from the south. This was planning on the largest scale, and soundly conceived. It was eventually to bring success to the Federal cause; but its initial moves were by no means faultlessly executed. Neither Sigel's advance down the Shenandoah nor Butler's thrust on Richmond met with success, while Meade's advance was skilfully opposed by Lee. Although Meade was nominally in charge of this attack on Richmond from the north in which the Iron Brigade participated, Grant by being present took over command, and Meade's headquarters became merely a post-office for Grant's instructions. Because of this the difficulties met with must be considered as the responsibility of Grant himself, just as the Iron Brigade considered that he was their real commander in the battles preceding the siege of Richmond and Petersburg.

It began for them on 3 May 1864, and because of its continuity was to be like no other campaign they had experienced. Gone were the days of sporadic fighting. War was now constant, and the two great armies fought for a year without being out of gunshot. Moving from their winter quarters, the Iron Brigade under General Cutler crossed the Rapidan at Germanna Ford and marched towards the Wilderness. There Lee got the better of Grant. He avoided being outflanked and eventually slipped away. After entering the forest Grant's army was struck by three Confederate corps moving from the west. Thus it turned, with Sedgwick's VI Corps, Warren's V Corps and Hancock's II Corps in line to meet them. Southwest of Wilderness Tavern where Grant had his headquarters, Warren's Corps faced Ewell's and Hill's; and the Iron Brigade on the right came to grips with Ewell's men with whom they had already crossed swords at Brawner Farm and Second Bull Run. The nature of the forest turned this battle into a slogging match which one of Hancock's brigadiers described as follows:

'As for the Wilderness, it was uneven, with woods, thickets and ravines right and left. Tangled thickets of pine, scrub-oak, and cedar prevented our seeing the enemy, and prevented anyone in command of a large force from determining accurately the position of the troops he was ordering to and fro. The appalling rattle of the musketry, the yells of the enemy, and the cheers of our own men were constantly in our ears. At times, our lines while firing could not see the array of the enemy, not fifty yards distant. After the battle was fairly begun, both sides were protected by log or earth breastworks.'

Grant conducted the operations personally, but they did not go as he wished, for the Confederates held his men in the woods, and he was unable to work round the Confederate east flank as he had planned. His headquarters near Wilderness Tavern were only half a mile behind the breastworks of the Iron Brigade, and when Warren's Corps was forced back some of the stragglers came into contact with their Commander-in-Chief. They were making their way to the rear while enemy shells were falling on the knoll where General Grant was seated on the stump of a tree. It looked as if the

George H. Stevens, Second Wisconsin (State Historical Society of Wisconsin)

Colonel Lucius Fairchild, Second Wisconsin

tide of battle would sweep over that point of the field, and the stragglers were amazed to see their leader smoking a cigar apparently quite unconcerned. Hancock's Corps was forced back as well as Warren's and a dangerous gap developed between the two formations; but both fought back staunchly. During this period the Iron Brigade was conspicuous and suffered severe casualties. Then Burnside at last managed to bring his three divisions forward and plug the gaps. From the tactical view the Wilderness battle was a draw, but strategically it ended in the favour of the North, for Lee withdrew afterwards to a position at Spottsylvania.

At Spottsylvania the Confederates occupied a strong salient position with a particularly well-defended point known as 'the Mule Shoe' or 'Bloody Angle' at the north end. In the battle which followed the Iron Brigade attacked on the west flank of the salient, and again were in the thick of the fighting, and suffered casualties. At Spottsylvania the Second Wisconsin, the oldest regiment in the Iron Brigade left. Reduced to fewer than 100 men, it was detached to become provost guard for the Division. The Second Wisconsin had an unsurpassed record during its three years of service, and suffered more casualties than any regiment in the Union armies. Those men who had not signed on for the duration were sent home to muster out, and the remainder, used for the provost guard, were formed into two companies. These were given the new title of Independent Battalion Wisconsin Volunteers, and the distinguished name Second Wisconsin Volunteers disappeared from the roster of the Army.

From Spottsylvania Grant thrust southward moving round the east flank of Lee's armies which conformed their movements to his. At the North Anna the armies met head on, and again the Northerners swung round to the east, moving to Bethesda Church and Cold Harbour. At Cold Harbour elements of Butler's force joined with Meade's in unsuccessful and costly assaults on the Confederate fortifications east of Richmond, but the Iron Brigade was not involved. Between Richmond and Petersburg, 20 miles south, the meandering River James, the River Appomattox and the extensive Confederate fortifications combined to provide a very strong defence line. To circumvent this Grant's armies bridged the James below its junction with the Appomattox and encircled Petersburg, moving gradually west and cutting the rail and road routes out to the south and south-west. With this the long siege of Petersburg began, both sides occupying trenches close to each other around the town. The onset of the siege permitted the results of the last six weeks of fighting to be assessed, and it was found that the Federals had lost more than 50,000 men in the Wilderness and following encounters – and the Iron Brigade, 902.

The Iron Brigade regiments, less the Second Wisconsin, remained in the trenches at Petersburg for several months. The siege was marked by a series of Federal thrusts in the south aimed at one or other of the rail and wagon roads supplying the Confederate Army. Among these, all involving bitter fighting, were four in which the Iron Brigade – now led by General Bragg – participated: the Battle of Globe Tavern in August 1864; Boydton Plank Road in October; a raid on the Weldon Railroad in December; and the Battle of Hotcher's End in early February 1865. Each of these engagements further weakened the strength of what remained of the once powerful regiments, adding 247 more of the Western soldiers to the long lists of casualties.

Bullets were not the only forces at Petersburg which struck at the remaining identity of the regiments of the Iron Brigade. There were frequent reorganizations and consolidations. On 25 August 1864 the 4th Division to which they belonged was broken up, and the Iron Brigade regiments were absorbed in the 3rd Division. The terms of those men of the Nineteenth Indiana, and the Sixth and Seventh Wisconsins who had not signed on now expired, and they left to be mustered out. One good which came out of this was that the old Second, now the Independent Battalion Wisconsin Volunteers, was merged with the depleted Sixth Wisconsin; but on the bad side, the Nineteenth Indiana was merged with the Twentieth, and lost its identity and left the Iron Brigade. These changes caused considerable resentment. It is recorded that there were 'long faces and much murmuring among our boys'; and one soldier is said to have exclaimed: 'It was a cruel act to separate and take them from the Old

Brigade; they left us, their hearts filled with sorrow over their forced separation from us; we felt badly over their being taken away, we all gloried in the record of the Iron Brigade, a record which they helped to make.'

Four months after the disappearance of the Nineteenth Indiana it was time for another regiment of the Iron Brigade to go. On 10 February 1865 Grant ordered Meade to send north some of his old reliable and reduced regiments to take charge of camps of newly drafted men at Baltimore; and Meade chose the Iron Brigade for this duty. General Crawford, the Divisional Commander, objected strongly to this, and asked to retain the Sixth and Seventh Wisconsin and Twenty-fourth Michigan, saying that he had a surplus of regiments which could much better be spared. 'The three regiments mentioned,' he said, 'have served together from the beginning of the war, and are identified with the Army of the Potomac. They desire to remain, and I ask the privilege of sending other regiments in their place.' General Warren, Commander V Corps, supported Crawford in his plea, adding, 'I have many regiments better fitted for service out of this army, and ask to be allowed to retain my Western regiments.' This strong appeal was not without effect, for although the Twenty-fourth Michigan was ordered to leave, both the Sixth and Seventh Wisconsin were permitted to remain.

For a time after the departure of the Twenty-fourth Michigan the Sixth and Seventh Wisconsin, commanded by Colonel John A. Kellogg of the Sixth, had the Brigade to themselves; but in March they were joined by the Ninety-first New York Volunteers, a heavy artillery unit that had been converted to infantry. With a large influx of Wisconsin recruits the arrival of the New Yorkers increased the total strength to over 3,000, so that the Iron Brigade under Colonel Kellogg ended the war in something like its old style.

The Federals now began a final thrust to break into Petersburg and at the same time block the escape routes of the much weakened enemy. Heavy Federal pressure was placed all along the line nearly enclosing the town. On 1 April 1865

Edward S. Bragg, Sixth Wisconsin (State Historical Society of Wisconsin)

John Azor Kellogg, Sixth Wisconsin (State Historical Society of Wisconsin)

the cavalry under General Sheridan – with the famous General Custer as one of his divisional commanders – together with V Corps, defeated the Confederates at Five Forks and closed the final escape route south of the Appomattox River. On the next day further assaults caused the enemy to start evacuating Petersburg. Fighting with the V Corps in their battles, the Iron Brigade played an important part in these successes, but the Sixth and Seventh Wisconsin lost a further 200 men in the process.

From Five Forks, the Iron Brigade followed in pursuit of the fleeing enemy along the Appomattox River, and at length, on the night of 8 April 1865, went into bivouac a few miles from Appomattox Court House. On the following morning the Iron Brigade resumed its advance, noticing as the day wore on that the sound of firing ahead had ceased. On the last morning the column halted again short of Appomattox Court House. Then, in the afternoon, an eye-witness recalled 'We saw an officer come riding down the lines, his horse wet and covered with lather. As he passed along we saw that the boys' caps went up in the air and heard their cheers. As he came in front of us he shouted, "General Lee and army have surrendered to General Grant". We yelled for joy, for we knew the war was ended.' Thus for the survivors of the regiments which had formed the Iron Brigade the end finally came.

The Confederate armies were disbanded as they surrendered, and were allowed to drift home; but the soldiers of Meade marched to Washington for a grand review before being mustered out. On 23 May the Army of the Potomac marched down Pennsylvania Avenue with flags flying and colors unfurled. Moving with the artillery was Battery B with Captain James Stewart at its head. Many men from the Iron Brigade had served its guns for three years, and the records were to show that it had lost more men during the war than any other Union battery. Further back in the column came the Sixth Wisconsin, and included in its ranks were veterans of the old Second Wisconsin. In step with the men of the Sixth and Second Wisconsin were the Seventh Wisconsin, and behind again, disguised as Twentieth came some of the old Nineteenth Indiana. This was the last march of the Iron Brigade, a unit which had won much honour in many fields.

Rufus R. Dawes. His colourful career with the Sixth Wisconsin began at the age of twenty-two on a visit to Wisconsin, when he heard the call for volunteers. He raised a company of 100 men and took them on the train to Washington. As a Colonel at Gettysburg he made a brave counter-attack, stormed the railway cutting, and retired with 230 prisoners

The Plates

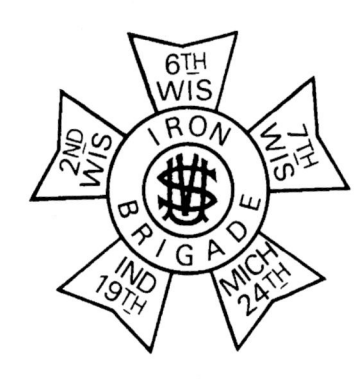

The first regiments of the Iron Brigade were undoubtedly clothed in volunteer grey, for in the Battle of First Bull Run Sherman is recorded as saying of the Second Wisconsin: 'This regiment was uniformed in grey cloth almost identical with that of the great bulk of the secession army, and when the regiment fell into confusion and retreated towards the road, there was a universal cry that they were being fired on by their own men.' In July 1861 when the Second Wisconsin, Nineteenth Indiana and Sixth Wisconsin were at Washington, the Sixth are said to have worn 'an all-grey short-jacketed uniform similar to that worn by the Second Wisconsin at Bull Run', and the Nineteenth Indiana arrived in Washington clad in 'gray doeskin cassimere'.

The next stage, for some of the regiments at least, was to wear the blue blouse and *képi* common to the Federal Army. The Twenty-fourth Michigan on joining the Iron Brigade in July 1862 are recorded as wearing 'a uniform consisting of the typical *képi* and short dark blue blouse with light blue trousers'.

The uniform associated with the Iron Brigade, however, was that introduced at Fredericksburg by their commander John Gibbon. This consisted of the black dress regular's hat, the regular dark blue army frock, white leggings and white gloves. In the photograph on page 12 showing members of I Company of the Seventh Wisconsin, all the men are wearing tall black hats, many punched up high. The regular Hardee hat had the brim turned up on the left side and fixed with a brass eagle pin. I Company do not appear to have turned their hats up, and other photographs show that the brim was usually turned down, but sometimes turned up on the right or left at the wearer's discretion. The black plume worn on the hat by the regulars is not distinguishable in the photograph. The plumes being highly perishable may very well have quickly worn out. The traditional infantry

The Union charge through the Cornfield north of Dunker Church

brass horn and brass company letter above it are very much in evidence, and the light blue cord can be seen in at least some of the photographs. The Iron Brigade belonged to I Corps and are said to have worn the round red cloth circle badge of the Corps on their hats; but this does not appear in photographs. The officers seem to wear a lower crowned hat than the men, or even a *képi*. Their hats, however, carry plumes.

Unquestionably the dark blue frock-coat, trimmed at the collar and cuffs with light blue, was issued by Gibbon to his men at Fredericksburg. It also seems likely that this part of the uniform was not regularly replaced, for the photograph of I Company of the Seventh Wisconsin at Upton's Hill shows only a minority wearing it, the rest having short blue blouses.

The white leggings are not depicted in available photographs, yet they are certainly mentioned in Rufus Dawes's diary, for he says, 'The regiment was fully supplied with white leggings' and goes on to describe a prank played by the men on their Commanding Officer when they put white leggings on his horse. He also mentions that the Twenty-fourth Michigan wore white leggings, and that they had become badly soiled, and, although useful, were no longer ornamental. At any rate it appears that after a time the leggings were not reissued and, like the white gloves, disappeared.

Despite the distinction of the uniform of the enlisted men, the officers of the Iron Brigade do not appear to have dressed unusually. The photographs show them wearing single- or double-breasted dark blue frock-coats with either dark or light blue trousers. In the photograph on page 12, two of the officers standing in front are wearing light blue trousers, while the third wears dark blue. The men, on the other hand, including the sergeants and drummer, are all wearing light blue trousers.

A1 Infantryman, Second Wisconsin, 1861
There was hardly time to train and equip the volunteer brigades before General McDowell led his army south in response to the Northern impatience to 'end the war'. This infantryman has been under arms for barely two months, and is dressed in the 'volunteer grey' – blouse jacket, trousers and *képi* all grey – with which he was issued by the State of Wisconsin before departing to Washington in June 1861. The accoutrements which can be seen in this picture – cartridge pouch, water-bottle and bayonet – are normal Federal issue.

A2 Infantryman, Nineteenth Indiana, 1861
In the first week of August 1861 the Nineteenth Indiana arrived in Washington clad in uniforms of 'gray doeskin cassimere', a fine twilled cloth of wool, and carrying an assortment of Enfield and Minié rifles, though these were shortly replaced with Springfield rifled muskets. The man here is doing sentry in foul weather, clad in a gum sheet and regulation Union *képi*.

A3 Infantryman, Sixth Wisconsin, 1861
The first company of Sixth Wisconsin Volunteers to muster in Madison, even before the Second Wisconsin had departed for Washington, arrived with 'grey hats trimmed with green' as their sole uniform. They were quickly issued with volunteer grey paid for by the State. The tenth and last company to arrive wore no uniform at all and were so undrilled that they were permitted to walk at their own gait. The man pictured here after his arrival in Washington has his State issue trousers, but has now been issued with a regulation greatcoat, and bears a Springfield rifle.

B1 Drummer, Rufus King's Brigade, 1861
When the Nineteenth Indiana departed from Indianapolis for Washington they had to leave behind their band as the uniforms available were considered substandard. Federal uniform was issued in September, and the Volunteers could no longer be mistaken for Confederates except that many of them preferred the quality of the State issue and, like this bandsman, clung to their grey overcoats when they could. The regulation *képi* is the only obvious clue to his Union identity. They must have been a hard-worked corps while the volunteers were being drilled at Arlington during the winter of 1861–2.

B2 Infantryman, Rufus King's Brigade, 1861
Standing proudly in his regulation Union dark blue blouse and light blue trousers, and gripping his rifled musket, is this young soldier of King's Brigade of McDowell's Division of the Army of the

Potomac, to which the Second, Sixth and Seventh Wisconsin and the Nineteenth Indiana Volunteers were assigned. No one had thought of calling them the 'Iron Brigade' yet, for after hearing very few shots fired in anger they spent their first winter in camp on Arlington Heights, Virginia.

B3 NCO, Rufus King's Brigade, 1861
This rather scruffy sergeant was by no means an unfamiliar figure off parade, and even the officers could be much more careless of their appearance than is acceptable today. The tie is non-regulation, but it was not unknown to wear silk scarves and even floppy bow ties under a buttoned jacket. His pistol is placed butt forward for a right-handed draw.

C1 Infantryman, General Gibbon's Brigade, 1862
Here is the uniform Gibbon introduced shortly after his appointment to the command. The soldiers were uniformed and equipped like the majority of the Federal regulars except for the distinctive features of the tall black Hardee hats with feather, the single-breasted frock-coat reaching to the knees in place of the short blouse, the white gaiters and the gloves worn for dress. See the caption to the picture on page 8 for a full description of the hat. The coat is dark blue with light blue trimmings. The leggings proved unpopular, and partly because of this and partly because they so easily deteriorated and became dirty, they were discontinued within a year.

C2 Infantryman, General Gibbon's Brigade, 1862
At Fredericksburg in May 1862 John Gibbon was promoted and transferred from the artillery company Battery B to take over command of the Brigade on Rufus King's promotion to Divisional Commander. This soldier's *képi* indicates that he is pictured within a few weeks of the appointment, for Gibbon quickly introduced the change of uniform, the most distinctive item of which was the tall black hat. The young infantryman has cast aside his jacket and *képi* in the heat of battle, and is kneeling up to charge his musket, which was an act impossible to perform lying down.

C3 Senior Officer, General Gibbon's Brigade, 1862
Typical dress for an officer of the Union Army: long blue coat, dark blue trousers, red sash under belt and red tassel on sword-hilt, the *képi* often worn in favour of the conventional felt hat. Based on a photograph of Lucius Fairchild, Lieutenant-Colonel of the Sixth Wisconsin Volunteers.

D1 NCO, Iron Brigade, 1863
After the Battle of South Mountain in September 1862 in which the Brigade fought with great courage and distinction, either McClellan or Hooker referred to the men as having qualities of iron. The men seized with enthusiasm upon this description of themselves, and were soon known to the whole Army by the name with which they have continued to be known to history. The corporal pictured here is properly, even dutifully dressed, and has not followed his comrades' convention of taking liberties with the style of the hat, for it is correctly turned up on the left side and the feather is still intact. In the pouch in the small of his back he carries powder. The blue cord around the base of the hat crown can just be discerned.

D2 Junior Officer, Iron Brigade, 1863–4
Despite the distinctive appearance of the enlisted men, the Iron Brigade's officers did not wear anything unusual. This officer has the typical single-breasted coat, light blue trousers (they could have been dark blue) and the black felt officer's hat. But here he has introduced a personal touch, for the hat wears the 'punched-up' look suspiciously like his men's, and he has taken advantage of the licence to pin the brim up on the right instead of the regulation left. This picture gives the best view of the blue hat cords.

D3 Infantryman, Iron Brigade, 1863
If his companions can be different by turning up the brim on the right, this Westerner can go further by not turning it up at all. Perhaps he has lost the brass eagle pin; perhaps he just likes it that way.

E1 NCO, Hall's Battery, 1863
Hall's battery of Horse Artillery fought alongside the Iron Brigade at Gettysburg. This sergeant's uniform is trimmed in artillery red; he wears a sword on his left side; a pistol carried butt forward on his right side, to permit a left-handed draw, is hardly to be seen in this picture. The pouch carries cartridges for the pistol.

E2 Infantryman, Iron Brigade, 1863-4
This can be considered the classic Iron Brigade soldier, the hero of Fredericksburg, Chancellorsville and Gettysburg. Dressed for the march, he carries rifle, knapsack, blanket roll, water-bottle, bayonet and cartridge pouch. In the knapsack there are, or might still be, 'one overcoat, three pairs of pants, three to five pairs of stockings, two woollen shirts, one undershirt, and two pairs of shoes'. His frock-coat has become lost or worn out and along with about half his fellows he has reverted to the Federal blouse. Gaiters and gloves are now only a memory. But the black hat is still resolutely maintained.

E3 Artilleryman, Battery B, 1861-5
The artillery battery which was attached to the Iron Brigade from its inception already had a proud record dating back to 1821. Their uniform was the Federal dark blue coat and light blue trousers with red artillery trimmings on coat and red stripe down the trousers. This man carries the rammer, one end used for ramming the charge down the barrel of the gun, the other for cleaning the barrel.

F Artillery Officer, Battery B, 1861-5
This officer wears no distinctive Iron Brigade dress but looks like any other artillery officer of the Union Army. The sword scabbard hangs at his left side. The hat is nothing to do with the Iron Brigade's speciality, but is the conventional officer's black felt hat, sometimes worn with feathers but often not. Single-breasted coat, dark blue trousers, knee-length riding boots.

G Mounted officer, Iron Brigade, 1861-5
As already stated, the officers of the Iron Brigade had no special tradition of dress, and could hardly be told apart from the rest of the Union Army.

H Officer, Buford's Cavalry, 1863
Buford's cavalrymen fought alongside the Iron Brigade at its greatest battle, Gettysburg, and justify their place here. The Cavalry arm is indicated by the yellow cord on the hat and the yellow stripe down the trousers. The sword placed for a right-handed draw would seem to put the pistol holster on the wrong side, but this man could very well have carried a holster on either side. It was not unknown for cavalrymen to carry four.

AFTERWORD

Originally called 'The Black Hat Brigade' because its men wore the regular army dress black hat instead of the more typical blue cap, the Iron Brigade was the only all-Western brigade that fought in the Eastern armies of the Union. Composed initially of the Second, Sixth, and Seventh Wisconsin Volunteers, and the Nineteenth Indiana Volunteers, the brigade also later included the Twenty-fourth Michigan Volunteers. Battery B of the Fourth U.S. Artillery, composed in large part of infantry men detached from the brigade, was not a part of the brigade but was closely associated with it.

It is fair to say that the Iron Brigade was perhaps the most distinguished infantry brigade in all of the Federal armies during the Civil War. The brigade's distinctions were several. In the first place, its Western origin marked it. It was also unusual because of its dress. But these two characteristics would have been immaterial had it not been for the brigade's final claim: it singled itself out by its valorous conduct. As a result of this conduct, stimulated perhaps by its unique origin and dress, the brigade suffered a greater percentage loss in men killed or mortally wounded than any other brigade in the Federal armies.

The brigade's distinctions – geographical origin, dress and conduct – were eloquently stated years ago by a soldier from another distinguished Federal organization, Berdan's United States Sharpshooters. Writing after the war and referring to the Federal retreat from Chancellorsville, Berdan's man described what happened when the Iron Brigade marched by other elements of the Federal army:

". . . as the great Western or Iron Brigade passed, looking like giants with their tall black hats, they were greeted with hearty cheers . . . And giants they were, in action . . . I look back and see that famed body of troops marching up that long muddy hill unmindful of the pouring rain, but full of life and spirit, with steady step, filling the entire roadway, their big black hats and feathers conspicuous . . ."

These are the stirring soldiers with which this book is concerned and I am pleased to provide an afterword. It is appropriate that a professional soldier has interested himself in the Iron Brigade and it is appropriate for Englishmen to learn more about an historic American military organization. The author's description, both in words and pictures, is worthy of the Iron Brigade.

Alan T. Nolan

Indianapolis, Indiana
Spring, 1971

INDEX

Figures in **bold** refer to illustrations. Colour plate letters are followed by caption page numbers in brackets.

Allen, Thomas S. **32**
Antietam, Battle of 14–16, **14**, **15**
Appomattox Courthouse 36
Appomattox River 34
Artillery officer **F** (40)
Artilleryman **E** (40)

Banks, General 8
Battery B 6, 11, 13, 14, 16, 17, 18, 19, 20, 21, 23, 28, **31**, 32, 36, 40
Beauregard, General 3, 4
Berdan's United States Sharpshooters 40
Bragg, General 34, **35**
Brawner Farm Battle **6**, 9
Buford, 27, 40
Bull Run, First 3–5, **5**, 37
Bull Run, Second 11
Burnside, Genenral Ambrose 13, 14, 16, 18, 21, 34

Callis, John B. **25**
Butler, General 32, 34
Chancellorsville 7, 21–25
Couch, General 24
Crawford, General 35
Cutler, Colonel Lysander 7–8, 10, 16, **17**, 20, 27, 30, 32, 33

Davis, President Jefferson 13
Dawes, Major Rufus 15, 27, 28, 29–30, 31, **36**, 38
Doubleday, General 9, 10, 17, 18
Drummer **B** (38)
Dudley, William W. **28**
Dunker Church **15**, 37

epaulettes 21
Ewell, General 10, 11, 28, 33

Fairchild, Colonel Lucius 30, **33**
Falmouth 6, 8, 16, 17
Fourteenth Brooklyn 22, 23
Franklin, 16, 17, 18, 20, 22
Frederick 13
Frederick's Hall 5–8, **7**, **8**
Fredericksburg 3, 6, 8, **18**, **19**, 22, 24, 37, 38
frock-coat 37, 38

Gettysburg 25–29, **30**, **31**, 39
Gibbon, Major John 6, **7** 8, 9, 10, 11, 12, 13, 14, 16, 17, 37, 38, 39
gloves 37, 38
Grant, General Ulysses S. 28, 31–32, 33, 34, 35
Groveton 8–11, **10**

Hancock, 34
Harper's Ferry 16

hats, black 6, **8**, 21, 25, 37, 39, 40
Henry House Hill 4, 12
Hill, A. P. 16, 33
Hood, 15, 28
Hooker, General 'Fighting Joe' 13, 14, 16, 17, 18, 21–22, 23, 24, 26, 39
Howard, General 28

Independent Battalion Wisconsin Volunteers 34
Indian people 30
Infantrymen **A** (38–39), **B** (38–39), **C** (39), **D** (39)
Iron Brigade: components 5–6, 40; distinctions 40; military efficiency 6; name 14, 26, 40; reorganization 34; uniform 6, 37–38

Jackson, General Stonewall 4, 6, 8, 9, 10, 11, 14, 18, 19, 24

Kellogg, John Azor **35**
képi 37, 38
King, General Rufus 5, 6, **6**, 9, 10, 39

Lee, General Robert E. 13, 14, 16, 17, 24, 25, 27, 33, 34, 36
leggings, white 37, 38
Lincoln, President Abraham 6, 13, 17
Longstreet, General 11, 12, 13, 28

McClellan, 13, 17, 39
McDowell, General Irvin 3, **3**, 4, 5, 6–7, 11, 38
Manassas 3, 4, 9, 10, 27
Maryland Campaign 13–16
Meade, General 17, 18, 19, 26, 27, **27** 32, 34, 35
Meredith, Brigadier-General Solomon 16, **19**, 21, 22, 26, 30
Morrow, Colonel Henry A. 16, 19, **20**, 30

N.C.O. **B** (39), **D** (39), **E** (40)
NCOs' chevrons **23**
New York Sharpshooters 30, 32
Nineteenth Indiana 5, 9, 10, 11, 13, 14, 15, 16, 20, 21, 27, 28, 34, 36, 37
Ninety-first New York Volunteers 35

O'Connor, Colonel 10, **10**
Officer, Junior **D** (39)
Officer, Mounted **G** (40), **H** (40)
Officer, Senior **C** (39)

Pelham, Major 18
Petersburg 32, 34, 35, 36
pistols **26**
plumes 37

Plummer, Captain 7, 8
Pope, General John 6, 7, 8, 9, 10, 11, 13
Porter, General 11
Potomac, Army of 7, 25, 26, 32, 35, 36
Potomac River 13, 14

Randall, Governor 5
Rapidan River 22, 24, 32
Rappahannock River 3, 9, 16, 22, 25, 31
Reynolds, General 22–23, 24, 27, 28, **30**
Richardson, Hollon **28**
Richmond 3, 6, 13, 16, 21, 31, 32, 34
rifles **26**, 38
Robinson, Colonel 10

Second Wisconsin 3, **4**, 5, 11, 16, 23, 27, 30, 34, 36, 37
Sedgwick, 22, 24, 33
Seventh Wisconson 5, 11, **12**, 13, 14, 15, 18, 24, 27, 30, 34, 35, 36, 38
Sharpsburg 13
Sheridan, General 36
Sherman, 32
Sherman, General William 4
shoulder bars **22**
Sigel, General 32
Sixth Wisconsin 5, 7, 11, 13, 14, 22, 23, 27, 28, 29, 30, 31, 34, 35, 36, 37
Spottsylvania 7, 8, 34
Stevens, George H. **33**
Stewart, Lieutenant 20, 21, **31**, 32, 36
Stoneham, General 22
Stuart, Lieutenant Jeb 7, 9, 18
Sumner, Edwin Vose 14, 16, 17, 18, 20, 21

Taliaferro, General 10
Third Indiana Cavalry 7
Twenty-fourth Michegan 5, 16, 17, 18, 19, 21, 22, 23, 24, 27, 30, 35, 37, 38
Tyler, General 4

uniforms 6, 37–38

Virginia 29, 32:
    Army of 6, 7

Wadsworth, General James S. 4, 22, 23, 24, 26, 27, 32
Warren, General G. K. 32, 33, 34, 35
Washington 3, **4**, 5, 13
Wilderness 22, 23, 24, 33
Wisconsin 3

41